Diary of an Optimist

Diary of an Optimist

Mary Barnard

*'Before I was married I had six theories about children;
after I was married I had six children and no theories.'*

John Wilmot, Earl of Rochester 1647-1680

The Larks Press

Typeset and published at
The Larks Press
Ordnance Farmhouse
Guist Bottom, Dereham, Norfolk NR20 5PF
01328 829207

Printed at the Lanceni Press
Fakenham, Norfolk

October 1995
Reprinted February 1997

British Library Cataloguing-in-Publication Data.
A catalogue record for this book is available in the British Library.

Contents

To Norwich

Southend-on-Sea
September 1948

James came striding in this morning with a broad grin on his face and a conspiratorial look in his eye, which if I hadn't been married to him for seven years I'd have said was a wheedling kind of look. But James never really wheedles. He just states. Today however he did seem particularly affable, and I had the sneaking feeling that something was afoot. Sure enough, something was. He sat down and in deliberate fashion lit his pipe.

'How would you like to live in Norfolk?'

'Why Norfolk for heaven's sake? We've only just got to Southend.'

'Well, I could think of several reasons,' said he, looking meditatively at the ceiling. 'A nice dry climate, nearer the two Grannies, still an easy train journey to London...'

'And...?'

'More job experience...'

'Ah! You mean you've applied for a post there.'

'Yes.' James was always direct.

'But you always said East Anglia was out of the main stream of progress; what has suddenly made you change your mind?'

'Promotion: a better salary. And the fact that Norwich is a lovely city.'

'Oh! so it's Norwich.'

'Yes. Are you coming?'

I should by now have been prepared for such shotgun propositions, but for once I hesitated.

'If you want an answer straight away it will probably be no, because you promised that the next move would be where there were hills, south or west. I'm tired of tussocky flat fields full of Fenland cows, I was born among them. And then of course there's the baby.'

But even as I said it I knew the baby could as easily be born in Norwich as here, or in Nairobi where the last move was mooted, or Timbuctoo. Babies just come regardless, though not always with comfort. (Very seldom with comfort if you think it over, but that wasn't quite the point.) Here in Southend at least a bed was booked for the event.

'What is this particular job, James?'

1

'Deputy Treasurer to the Corporation. And there's a house to go with it. At least,' seeing my sudden interest, 'a part of a house. Of a mansion actually, divided into three flats. But once in Norwich of course we could look for a place of our own.'

M'm. That meant two moves, and against them the desire to stay put was strong.

My hesitation was well-founded: life with James has always been a switchback, and I have often wondered, dreaming over the soap-suds or scraping the eternal nappies, how I came in my thirties to be permanently established between sink and cot, pandering to three wriggling, stimulating offspring and a fourth imminent: I, the once career girl with the world to choose from, thinking vaguely of promotion and only half in love with marriage, and even that depending more on the person than the institution. Children weren't in the picture at all. Children were those hopeful, keen-eyed, maddening guardians of the future, often a joy to teach, but nothing to do with the kitchen sink, and certainly nothing whatever to do with nappies.

So what reason for the change of direction?

James, of course. And the war, one can't leave out the war. But it was, eventually, James's persuasive grin, and his idealism and his lightning decisions, that changed the even pattern of my life. James grew on one.

When we met he was a would-be seminarian, a celibate, and to a Catholic, an untouchable. It was only later after he had given up the idea of the seminary that he became that rare bird in local government, a mediaeval historian turned municipal accountant. He had gone up to Oxford on a diocesan scholarship, backed by his father, to become an Anglican priest. Who knows, perhaps the more he probed into his subject the nearer he felt to Rome, though he fought it every inch of the way, but to everyone's consternation he left Oxford a Catholic, and, what is more, engaged to one, to the girl next door to his lodgings. This both upset the family applecart and removed his career in the Anglican ministry. So, feeling the need to placate his father and find himself a job, James became articled in local government, which sacrifice meant three years without pay.

In time, still cherishing his ideal of the priesthood, which now would be a celibate one, he broke off his engagement to the girl next door and applied for a place at the Jesuit seminary in Oxford. The waiting proved long, so endeavouring to make something of this temporary life, once his articles were finished, James moved to Peterborough and there caught up with our family.

I never met her, but I have always had great admiration for the girl who gave him up.

✝ ✝ ✝

My sister Anne and I were both intrigued by this strapping young man who seemed to have one foot in the church and the other in the Borough Treasurer's office. We welcomed James as befitted a future celibate, took him punting, plied him with theological argument and my mother's apple tarts and waited to see what happened next.

What did happen seemed on the surface another sudden decision, although in retrospect I realised it was the result of much prayer and agony of mind, combined with the realisation that the petit mal from which he suffered would always be a barrier to his ordination. The timing was crucial, being the culmination of the long tense months of the Cold War of 1939 with the paralysing threat of war blotting out any thoughts of a future. Austria, Czechoslovakia and Poland were already annexed by Hitler, obviously intent on subjugating Europe. James met me as usual one day by the river and told me he was abandoning the seminary and how about us getting married.

My first astonished reaction was followed by a deep sense of guilt; had I lured James from his natural destiny? And what future was there for any of us anyway, the Nazis now occupying Denmark and Norway and heading for France and the Low Countries? And, nearer to the heart of things, could this pleasant affectionate relationship mature to one of lasting loving commitment? In the following months of indecision I came to know that it could, and that I needed to share whatever was coming with James, annihilation though it might be. There was really nothing to wait for, and we became engaged in the actual month that the Nazis marched into France, Holland and Belgium, May 1940.

May 1940

It was a gut-knotting time. I looked around at the yellow meadows and the hedges clotted with hawthorn in that most beautiful May, with

3

summer and its lazy days almost upon us, thinking that the enemy could only obliterate what was pushing up through the earth, never the deep roots themselves, and that green life would flourish again in the years to come when all this was over, a thought that at the time must have seemed naïve, or at least overly hopeful. But I was always an optimist and felt that in the earth as in the hearts of men there is continuity and I could not conceive the annihilation of either.

So the human spirit being fairly irrepressible, and James being turned down for the army (he was by now auditor to the Wellingborough Urban District Council), we were married within the year. Having behind us the vast sum of forty pounds, entirely saved by James, we set up house on the edge of the Midlands. There, nine months later, amid rationing and utility furniture, Nicola was born.

‡ ‡ ‡

It was the utility furniture that rankled with Nana Loomes, my mother, and I had to admit that without the Victoriana she had so nobly given us we should hardly have been furnished at all.

'You might as well have the stuff now,' said she practically, 'because you'll be getting it anyway when I'm gone. Look at the workmanship of these pieces,' running her hands expertly over a massive chest of drawers, 'you don't get it like that these days.'

She had married in turn two middle-aged bachelors, both pillars of society, and some of her wedding presents had been very fine, though somewhat convoluted, examples of Victorian craftsmanship. She not unnaturally despised what was being served up as furniture in wartime.

'What do you get now?' she snorted. 'Utility! The name just about sums it up; stuff that's useful and nothing more. Now feel these,' pulling out two drawers at once, 'proper drawers that run at a finger touch. And look at this solid overmantel and this delicate carving...'

'Bit of a dust-trap...'

'Dust? Who cares about dust? It's craftsman-made, that's the point. Mr Pettit would turn in his grave if he saw the stuff you have to put up with nowadays...'

She spoke more in sadness than in anger. Mr Pettit had been her first husband, who had provided the furniture, a portly bearded gentleman looking like Edward VII, whose Christian name was William, though

4

never in all the years I had known her had she ever called him that. I wondered if the term was perhaps too intimate.

She returned to the attack.

'Look at this canopy bed now.' We looked; it was firmly planted by now in our front bedroom, another Victorian masterpiece, in a warm golden maple, its long green curtains hiding a load of clobber.

'That used to be draped in scarlet repp, backcloth, curtains and valance, fifteen yards of it. And lined. Mr Pettit had a little scarlet pocket made to hang on the backcloth just big enough to hold his gold watch at night. And you know there's a key to dismantle the bed in a special hiding-place,' and to underline it firmly she flipped open a panel in the bedpost and there it was stowed away inside.

My mother was, in spite of her eccentric ways and somewhat peremptory manner, a great supporter; she backed us stoutly all through the war when we were in far-flung parts of England furthering James's career. In those days we were unknown to the local tradesmen and were merely faces in a queue, so she would send us rare delicacies like glucose ('to keep up your energy'), or chocolate bars or tins of saved-up corned beef, much of it obtained by being at the grocer's at the right time. We always took her word for this, for though she would never descend to the black market, being a magistrate, she would have a whale of a time in the grey.

Nana had visited us faithfully during our various journeyings in Wellingborough, Stockton-on-Tees, Southend, bringing us goodies in the dark days, sitting-in for the births of the babies, bringing us a taste of a less confined life and forbearing to comment on our sudden removals from one town to another, which must to her have seemed without rhyme or reason in the middle of a war. (It often seemed that way to me too.) In fact I was constantly amazed that none of the three children was ever born in a furniture van. Every time we were expecting another child it seemed that James got the urge for promotion and off we went to somewhere new, regardless of the fact that we were working our way through the most widespread war in history, much of it on our doorstep. Usually we moved with discomfort to a far county, set up house in a strange town, registered with food suppliers who had no real interest in our needs and I would pour it all out in yet another diary to add to all the rest. In this way, in three moves and seven years, rather as in a protracted game of chess, we arrived and have even stayed awhile in Southend.

† † †

I have enjoyed Southend. It is a melting pot of east-, west- and middle-enders like us. Here there is a camaraderie, a kind of bawdiness, a natural optimism for ever bubbling up among the people in the streets. There is a love of the sort of food that most of us have forgotten, cow's heel, pig's foot, tripe, jellied eels, whelks, which have everything to do with nourishment but not much with haute cuisine. Southenders have an urge for a gamble which has no relation to income, and a stalwart sense of humour which defies a post-war austerity. I enjoy the crowds from the East End of London milling around the tripe-and-onion stalls and the candy-floss kiosks and the pier, though I can get as nettled as the next mum when I try to push the pram through a wedge of Stepney matrons with 'Kiss me Quick' streamed across their paper hats. But in winter when the Londoners come no longer, when the cockle stalls are closed and fish and chip papers blow moodily past Ernie's Oyster Bar, I miss them all, even though I can push the pram right up the High Street without interference.

In summer the climate is near perfect, the town being on an estuary facing south. You can walk for miles at low tide wriggling your toes in sea-mud and yet never find the sea, only eternal sand-patterns and cockles. Nana Loomes, on her sporadic visits to her grandchildren, our three red-haired delinquents, Nicola, Roger and Sue, loves Southend. She takes the little train to the end of the pier and sits under the furthermost shelter, sunning herself. I believe she feels she is at sea, relaxing there all day with a bar of chocolate and a cup of tea, and then taking the train back one-and-a-third miles to the starting-point, to where her heroine, Queen Victoria, stands forever frozen in stone, pointing with her sceptre to the public conveniences.

October 8th 1948

Here at home events are hotting up; the joint decision has been made and we are off to Norfolk after all. James has accepted the post of deputy Treasurer to Norwich City Council and takes it up in six weeks' time. He now comes home with all sorts of newsy items which he hopes will gild the pill of upheaval.

'The house,' says he, 'is in one of the pleasantest parts of the city in a wide road with trees. There's a nursing-home opposite and a hospital up the road. What's more they say you can go up and look it over, just to see if you approve.'

Look it over and approve! A rare privilege indeed with everyone scrambling for houses after the bombing. It might be a civilised move after all. James, sensing this, grins and pushes home his previous argument that at least this will get us there and later we can look round for something else. This sort of argument seems to me familiar.

'You really promise that?'

'Cross me heart.'

I take it for what it is, a mixture of hope and good intentions.

So we uproot once more, this time for a city only two hours' journey from where I was born. New job, new baby, new diary, and removals all over again.

Removals, I regret to say, are a sore point with me. It isn't that I don't enjoy organising them but events never row in with me; as with inanimate objects they have a hostility of their own. Take the move we made from Wellingborough to Stockton-on-Tees, which was not helped by it happening in the last year of the war. I was given four days to pack up. We had evacuees in the back bedroom, a blonde Lithuanian cockney and five-year-old boy, with husband at weekends. The new buyer asked to sleep at ours until the furniture went, as her drunken landlord was making unpleasant advances. It rained solidly for the four days, so that two-year-old Nicola caused mayhem around our infant Roger while I stacked up. We even gave a farewell dinner party. Moreover, having packed, James decided to leave the whole set-up to the occupants for a week so that we might take his overdue holiday in Suffolk, on the principle I suppose that if he didn't take it then, he would lose it altogether, and that meanwhile one set of occupants would keep an eye on the other.

Miraculously it worked. The evacuees, civilised folk, saw off the furniture for us and the load arrived in Stockton intact. James, travelling in advance, also arrived intact. It was the rest of us who were casualties.

A travel-grimed quartette, to wit, James's sister Constance, Nicola Roger and myself, arrived at a blitzed station in the North-East in a cloudburst. From this gushing welcome a taxi deposited us on our new doorstep, not the front, I hasten to say, but the back, the front door key being missing. From a large van waiting on the kerb a somewhat disgruntled man ambled up with a piece of paper in his hand. 'Bin waiting here an hour,' he said. 'Guv'nor said twelve o'clock.'

'Couldn't you have started unpacking?' I asked briskly. 'The neighbours have a key to the kitchen door.'

'Oo-oh, no, couldn't do that, love. Little matter of £33 to be settled. Can't unload till I get it.'

Good grief, where was James? It was still pouring with rain, a state I came to associate with the north-east for many months; the baby wanted feeding and the man was agitating. Had James been detained at the office? Or mistaken the time? Been run over? Or was it just the wrong day? But just as I'd decided I should have to sit on the drive and feed Roger, the taxi having long gone, James himself came smiling up the path, unflappable as ever, and broke to us the rest of the good news.

He'd done some reconnoitring. There was no gas stove; up north they take it with them. None of the electric sockets would take our plugs, so we should have to cook on a coal fire. But there was no coal, it was rationed, and there was only a bucketful borrowed from neighbours. The bedding was wet from the long wait in the van with the back down and Nana's famous key to assemble the bed was missing. The blackout blinds didn't fit, so that we couldn't even use candles for lighting for fear of showing a gleam, and we hadn't yet registered for milk, coal or groceries. And still it rained.

The first night we bedded Roger in a drawer, went to bed in the dark and slept on a mattress on the floor. We got up by the non-existent sun because the electric clock, our only timepiece, couldn't be plugged in.

The second day we got gas but not electricity.

On the third day we got milk, not our full allowance, for which we still weren't registered, but milk.

On the fourth day we were given a front door key and borrowed a clock as James going to work by the sun was unreliable. There wasn't any.

On the fifth day the plugs were all connected with the sockets except the clocks. 'No proper flexes on these wartime clocks,' complained the electrician. 'Now mine's a Ferranti, you oughter try one of them.' Good for Ferranti, I thought.

But on the sixth a bonanza: full ration of milk, fires plugged in; clock; coal. I felt in touch with Life again. It was then we realised we were two miles from the nearest grocer, here on our desirable modern housing estate surrounded by cornfields.

'Lucky you wasn't here during the blitz,' had said the Ferranti man. 'Lucky you got a house like this.'

Well, I had to admit it *was* a bonus; life behind the battle zone (if it could be said to have a behind) had for years been an unrelenting grind, that of the ground-down majority behind the reluctant heroes and no medals ever for the half-starved and bombed upon. For when I did push the children two miles in the big old secondhand pram there wasn't much bounty to be found there. The basic rations per person per week in September 1944 were two ounces of cheese, six of butter or margarine, one-and-tuppence worth of meat and four ounces of bacon and ham, with two ounces of tea for James and me and less than one egg each for the four of us (31 per year).

But yes, the house was a bonus: we could have been parted, or evacuated, or living with relations, in a pre-fab or half-bombed shell, whereas we were alive, unblitzed and together. Yet I couldn't help thinking as I surveyed our neat little dwelling on the edge of the windy fields that shops, doctors and bus-stops were as important as all mod. cons., and that next time perhaps I would inspect the terrain in advance.

The weather didn't help. It was October, I recall, before they cut the sodden corn.

October 17th

Acting on hard-won experience, I have been up to Norwich to see the flat. I need not have worried; Newmarket Road is all I had been led to expect, broad, spacious, dignified with trees, now flaring with all the colours of autumn. I could imagine a century ago the shoe barons and the mustard barons bowling down it of an evening in their carriages from the city, horses high-stepping down the avenue of trees, wheels flurrying the gravel of their drives; for this is a road of mansions. The tall chestnuts and elms must have been newly planted then and the white Costessey brick of the houses the colour of fresh milk in the evening light.

The wide road is pleasant still, but a little greyer. All the houses have stables lining their narrow back lanes, which are a feature of Norwich. Though horses and carriages have long since gone, the outhouses are still intact, rather overgrown and adapted now for cars, boat clobber and the hundred things a house can never take. Number eighty-four, Fernlea, is one of these. It stands square to the road, aproned by a circular lawn and with imposing neo-classical pillars. Even in its present state of half-repair it exerts authority. For the life of me I dared not walk across that lawn but instead stepped circumspectly round the edge. The overgrown garden is rampant with trees and shrubs and behind the house I found a lily pool, its fountain adrift in the shallows; behind that again a substantial kitchen garden. But what really warmed my imagination were the outhouses and shrubberies where the children could play Cowboys and Indians without ever being seen at all.

It seems that three families are to live in this paradise, a headmaster, an architect and ourselves. We share the first floor with the architect and have the run of the attics above. I climbed over saw benches and planks in the huge first floor living-room to look out of one of the windows and found myself on a level with the trees among the bronze and gold, so near that I could lean out and almost touch the startled birds. The attics above would be our bedrooms, reached by a narrow stair and sporting one high dormer window each. Here no doubt our predecessors put their maids, unintentionally ensuring that they had little light and no view. Peering on tiptoe, I could only see a chimney-pot, and James, exploring weird noises there one evening, came face to face with a large barn owl.

Altogether full of exciting possibilities. I wonder which third of the garden will be ours. A piece at the back, I hope. I am doubtful about the effect of a future four youngsters in a front garden on Newmarket Road. The descendants of the shoe barons don't know what they're in for.

October 20th

James has gone, absorbed into the fogs and 'digs' of Norwich. We at home are in the usual trough of coughs and colds and there is an implacable steel sky over the estuary that seems to cover the world. Possibly just a psychological greyness of mood after the euphoria of the last few weeks, for I find myself crippled with pain probably due to the baby. The doctor assures me that some surgical repair after the birth will be all that is needed and he will put me on the National Health list for an operation. Probably be some months yet, he adds cheerfully.

'Months?' I croak.

'Well, could be some years,' says he, 'but I'll give you some temporary support. Take life easy for the next six months.'

Take life easy! We move in four weeks!

I come home thoroughly maudlin and revive my flagging spirits with a couple of Southend kippers, knowing full well that the next job, packing up for the move, is upon me.

Fortified by the kippers and the last of the cooking sherry, I decide that this is the moment for an SOS to Nana Loomes.

October 25th

So I have persuaded Nana to come down and wash curtains, patch chaircovers and generally keep the place tidy for customers while I cope with the children. She has strict instructions to direct visitors round the front of the settee as the flowered cover doesn't quite stretch over the back, due to the fact that clothes rationing came in seven years ago and furnishing fabrics at several coupons per yard immediately disappeared from the market. This, as you would imagine, put a sharp stop to romantic white wedding dresses, mine having been one of the last before the clamp-down; Anne never got one at all. So we play Box and Cox: the curtains in one house become the sofa covers in another, and the green bedspreads of Wellingborough become the dining-room curtains of Southend.

'In short supply ...' is written on my heart, deeply, ineradicably.

However one lasting success was the turning of Nana's scarlet repp bed-curtains (circa 1904) into a maternity coat for me for the three babies; chunky and dramatic it camouflages the present incumbent even now.

'Made to last, that's why,' says Nana, vigorously machining patches on the settee seat. 'Beautiful stuff, repp, you could cut it like cheese. No fraying, stands up by itself.'

James is more phlegmatic. 'I can't think why you're bothering about loose covers,' says he. 'Nobody's buying the furniture.'

As he is in Norwich for the greater part of the week he won't be bothering about selling anyway. Meanwhile the rest of us remain here, unnaturally clean, awaiting our first customers.

‡ ‡ ‡

October 31st

Did I say customers? They are besieging us every hour. For some reason James has resorted to two means of selling simultaneously: an advertisement in the local paper and the services of Messrs Winchell

& Sons, estate agents. I find the advert-answerers are becoming over-ridden by the agents, who have the greater expertise and out-face me. For instance, at breakfast-time this morning a mother-of-four stood on the doorstep desperate to have a look round. I never mind mothers-of-four, they are comrades in arms, so she was whisked through the house without any preamble, approved of it straight away and I promised not to sell until her husband could come and see it.

At eleven o'clock Winchell's man arrived with a middle-aged couple, wife worried-looking and dressed in black. I place on record the sparring tactics that characterised the interview, for I realised quite early on that nothing was going to be right for the Middle-Aged Lady in Black.

'The house is about thirty years old,' I said casually, not minding much whether she had it or not, but pointing nevertheless to the solid foundations. 'Built somewhere about 1913.'

'Thirty years old?' echoed the M.A.L.I.B. dismally looking round immediately for woodworm and rot. 'Ooh, that's rather old, isn't it, Harold?'

'Could have been Georgian,' I answered crisply, 'then it would have been even older,' and the agent, sensing hostilities, hastily pointed out the remarkable depth of the skirting boards in this utility day and age.

'Well, come and see the bathroom,' I offered, leading the way firmly past the damp patch and the carpet-hole at the top of the stairs. 'Really quite spacious.'

'Oh dear, you want a new bath,' she wailed immediately. 'Look at this, Harold,' leading him to our very small patch of worn enamel. Let her *try* getting a new bath at the end of a war, I gritted to myself, but aloud said airily, 'Ah, but it has a bell for summoning the maid, should you get into difficulties.'

She didn't quite know how to take this, and was grudgingly quiet through the bedrooms, four nice sunny ones, and the next wail wasn't uttered until she got downstairs again, when from the depths I heard, '1913! Harold, it's more than thirty years old, it's thirty-five.'

Thus we filed, a pathetic little pilgrimage, round the remaining rooms. Everywhere something was wrong: the glass lean-to made the scullery dark; the greenhouse had no roof, thanks to Hitler, and her last despairing squeak came from the dining-room, where she was certain we had wood-rot. The evidence for this was the loose floorboard that covered the electrical wiring, but this time the agent was moved enough to take up the offending plank and get her to thrust her hand down and feel the wires. I thought bitterly that the lady with four children had asked no fatuous questions. She went once round the house, stood in the hallway and said, 'This'll do.' Besides which it was a pleasant seaside terrace house with glass front doors in addition to storm doors,a pocket handkerchief garden and the remains of a vine-filled conservatory.

I was amazed, after all this, when the M.A.L.I.B. turned round and begged me to let her have it. It seemed she had been let down by another seller at the moment of purchase and, having sold her own, was without a home.

I made a call to James in Norwich asking for his judgment on the sale. Was it to be my customer or the agent's? James plumped for the agent's. So, several pounds poorer for having sold it through Winchell's, I plonked Sue in the pram and went to break the news to my lady-with-four with whom I felt considerable affinity. But the decision rankled with me for days.

Norwich
November 23rd

We're here. Now at the end of November the family is together again, in the gracious first-floor living-room of Fernlea, up among the trees, and below the long attic bedrooms with the dormer windows. Certainly the aftermath of war drives us to unusual boltholes.

We moved in fog; Norwich being completely shrouded in it. Place-names and buildings appeared sharply in front of our noses and as quickly dissolved into the mist again; the garden trees dripped with perpetual raindrops and greyness enveloped everything. For the first few days it was a city of wraiths. Nicola and I tramped through the thick fog as soon as we arrived to fix her up at the Convent Preparatory School. We peered myopically at all the brass plates on all the porticoed buildings in Surrey Street until we reached a modern brown notice on a drive pillar, 'Convent of Notre Dame'.

There the door was opened on to the fog by a bright-faced, quizzical bird-like nun, Sister Celestine. She took me along corridors that smelled of beeswax and we finally conversed in a beautiful salon with tall arched windows and the longest walnut table I have ever seen, topped by a bowl of chrysanthemums. How easy to be good, I felt, in such gracious

13

surroundings, though knowing in my heart that the enemy is always within. Between chatting of this and that we arranged that Nicola should start straight away in a grey skirt and white blouse until the green uniform was ready.

Sister Celestine, as we said goodbye on the doorstep, was intrigued to hear that James was in the City Treasurer's department. 'I shall be haunting Room 114 at the City Hall,' said she, 'for I cannot, simply cannot, cope with these awful income tax forms.'

I didn't dare tell her that James didn't deal with income tax but Nicola, sensing that even nuns don't always receive divine inspiration and that someone in authority might even be human, skipped all the way home.

† † †

Once having settled in I am finding that things are done properly in this part of East Anglia. For one thing the provision shops and the buses are staffed by men, and the butcher and baker compete for custom, very different from the North or Southend, much as I loved them, where the bus conductors were clippies and the shop assistants snippies as often as not. Here even the travelling grocer is an ex-officer and without doubt a gentleman. The whole atmosphere is redolent of a bygone age, one carefully preserved perhaps by Norfolk's isolated position. Its motto, I hear, is 'Du different.' I was delighted too to find I could get some help in the house, an unheard-of luxury.

So Jeannie has joined the household, a stout country girl from the neighbouring village of Hethersett, cheerful, uninhibited but quite adept, having been occasional maid at the Hall there. For Jeannie, I gather, working for us is a form of slumming, but she tolerates us quite well and divides herself between us and a family further up the road.

'My other lady wouldn't have her coffee in the kitchen with me,' said Jeannie on her second visit, 'not like you. But I like working for you. I thought you'd be different somehow, from what Mr B. say when he interviewed me in his office. I liked Mr B., his suit and shirt looked so nice and I say to my friend, 'He's a smasher, but I expect she's little and clinging,' especially when I heard you was expecting your fourth.'

Jeannie agreed however after seeing me that I wasn't really the clinging type and I thought I detected a certain disappointment as if I hadn't quite made the grade. It reminded me of my pal Serena, who in her time had been at Girton but who later became submerged beneath five children somewhere in the North. Her help, Alice, confided over coffee one morning, no doubt also in the kitchen:

'You know that Mrs Golightly, mum, that I work for up the road? She knows how to do things properly. She's had a good education, been to Accrington Grammar School. Not like you, I know you never had a good education like that, but you do appreciate when someone's trying to help you out.'

‡   ‡   ‡

December 26th

Christmas here has been perhaps the most luxurious of all. It is then that the heart of Norwich comes alive. The huge fir tree given annually by the Norwegian people stands high on the City Hall steps ablaze with fairy lights, the faint tinkle of silver foil coming over thinly on the frosty wind. Below it the flare-lit market stalls with their coloured tilts line the alleys with bright pyramids of fruit, all kinds of

Roger

fruit. Not for years have I seen such a riot of oranges, lemons, grapefruit, bananas, holly and even hothouse flowers. In and out of the aisles the pedlars dangle their fur monkeys, tumbling clowns, yo-yos...

The children move through it as in a dream. It is all quite unlike the last wartime Christmas in the bleak North (only four years ago) when the youngsters were isolated with whooping-cough and not a soul came near us. Roger's most successful present then was a brightly painted scourer tin full of pebbles. James had bought a large Christmas tree and we managed to make it sparkle with soft silver stars cut out of milk tops, and with spiky gold ones from syrup tins, and with paper chains cut from the pictures in colour magazines and a few real electric lights. Money as well as toys was short in those days.

My last two red apples, I recall, went in the stockings. My sister Anne had made the children some dolls' house furniture out of matchboxes, one suite in lemon and green for the dining-room and one in orange for the bedroom, while the bedroom chest had real matchbox drawers that pulled out with boot-button handles. The pièce de resistance was a rocking

15

cradle with tiny bedding and peg dolls tucked away in it.

I enjoyed that Christmas because it was quiet and uneventful and this one because it wasn't. The little luxuries have come filtering back, the pot plants, the wine and most of all, the toys.

Nicola, now six, her eyes shining, runs about happily in not-so-utility clothes. In fact she is a changed child from the thin, tense little slip of a girl of earlier days and seems to be more contented, though I feel life may always hold some apprehension for her. Nicola grasps at life tentatively in all directions, rather like a sea-anemone in an undersea world, and just as easily do her tentacles retract. Criticisms scattered about in class and home always affect Nicola intensely, whether intended for her or not, and when the family is smitten with any sort of infectious disease it is she who suffers the most, emerging from it pale and waif-like.

Roger, at almost five quite a different kettle of fish, will start school for the first time here in Norwich. Nicola found the move rather traumatic but Roger will weather it better. At present he has picked up a swear word and goes round muttering, 'Silly bugger, silly bugger.' I reprimand him without putting too much emphasis on it so he has reverted to 'damn'. But now and again there is a confrontation. Father bought him a secondhand Hornby engine, precious because unobtainable, and he sold it to another boy in Southend for threepence. After the paternal explosion I thought it wise to try and get it back, so we had a little inquisition.

'Roger, how well do you know this boy who bought your engine?'

'Only a bit.'

'How much is a bit?'

'I met him in the street.'

'What's his name and what does he look like?'

'I think he's called William, an' he has sort of brown hair, reddish face, short trousers like mine, an' a school cap. I think...'

The original Just William from the sound of it.

'How is he different from any other boy?'

'He's got my engine.'

Not helpful.

'Could you show me where he lives then?'

'Yes.'

But he couldn't. We set out resolutely one afternoon to find him but after knocking on the sixth door ('I'm sure it was this one') we gave it up.

We just don't mention clockwork engines any more, and Roger has learnt an expensive lesson. Or perhaps we have.

Roger is always a realist. In a relaxed moment I asked the three of them what they would like the next baby to be, girl or boy.

'Girl,' said Nicola and Sue with one voice.

Roger squirmed. 'I'd sooner have a bag of sweets,' said he. 'A silly question, I suppose, deserves a silly answer.'

Sue at almost two is an independent little person, eternally exploring, trotting round from one object to another, grinning hugely, red curls rioting, drinking out of tin cans, jugs, emptying cupboards, teasing the cat and eating the soap. When Blackie the cat had kittens, Sue trotted in to me with a wet newborn kitten, squealed, 'Here y'are, Mummy,' and deposited it in my lap. On another occasion when we were visiting the farm of James's sister Joan in Suffolk, Sue suddenly saw the nine farm cats and kittens huddled in a heap in front of the Aga. Squealing with delight, she picked up the kittens by the fur, tails, legs or anything handy, squeezed them and hugged them and got into the heap with them. When the exhausted creatures finally curled up into a compact mass again she lay down on top of the lot and went to sleep herself. There seems to be a strong *Sue* maternal streak in Sue; perhaps we have a future materfamilias here.

† † †

Three weeks after Christmas Sue has had her second birthday and Roger has at last started school. He set off, brushed, polished and clean, with his name and address sewn on a tape inside his new coat, was drilled to repeat where he lived and had it all off pat, Fernlea-Newmarket-Road-Norwich. Clutching two-and-a-penny dinner money and a clean hanky he went off with Father to catch the bus. No-one quite knew how he would return, but the school and James's office being only a hundred yards apart we felt a word with the headmaster would be enough and a Big Girl would probably see him to the bus stop.

17

At four o'clock Roger walked beaming into Room 114 at the City Hall: 'The Big Girl didn't turn up, so I walked out.'

Father, slightly taken aback by this turn of events, delivered him into the hands of his secretary, who went down through the city with him to catch the bus.

This visit was immediately followed by another. The school head himself, finding Roger had disappeared, thought he too had better present himself at the City Hall to explain. Apologies all round. I felt we had created somewhat of a disturbance.

The next day Roger proved equally ingenious. Fired with the spirit of exploration and jingling his bus fare in his pocket, he walked a mile from school right through the busy city and caught a bus for the one last stop, fifty yards from home. I don't think we need worry about Roger's peregrinations any more.

January 1949

Following our settling-in came that stalwart trooper Nana Loomes. She drove up in a taxi to our palatial surroundings, argued with the driver that this could not possibly be the house; walked into the kitchen and started cooking her own vegetables ('Brought some brussels sprouts from that bed near the fowl pen. Just wasting while I'm away. What's this thing? Pressure-cooker? Never heard of it'); took a tin of mincepies out of a large chamberpot she'd brought with her on the train ('Yours aren't big enough, silly little things'; though whether she referred to pies or pot I knew not), and proceeded to create a maelstrom in the kitchen. Throughout the years I have never ceased to compare the doings of Nana Loomes with the making of candyfloss; she waves an imaginary wand and immediately where there was nothing at all there appear myriads of complicated strands.

She shuttled purposefully to and fro; I would like to say she pottered but my mother never potters, even at seventy-two.

'I've brought my own teapot too,' she said busily putting the stuff away, which really meant laying it all down, for Nana always worked on the principle that anything out of sight was out of mind and she might want them in a minute, an hour, tomorrow, next week. So some of the consignment was stacked on the flat top of the washer.

'Actually that's a washing-machine,' said I, 'and we do use it every day...'

18

'Every day? Huh, must wear the clothes out...'

'And in between washes it alternates as a dishwasher...'

'A dishwasher? What on earth's a dishwasher?'

'A gadget that washes dishes, that is if you've got the strength to change the tubs over.' It was an American machine and I can only conclude that American women are strapping great Amazons - due to all those steaks and no wartime rationing - for it was as much as I could do to lift the heavy washer tank out of its casing in order to put the other in. Perhaps unwise too at four months pregnant.

'Well, it's all beyond me,' said Nana, her face rueful for once. 'I've always boiled the clothes in the scullery copper, fire underneath, and rinsed them in the sink. No detergents, they came in with the war. Hudson's Dry Soap powder was all we had years ago, you shook it in... Or you scrubbed with a bar of soap. Lot of work: much better nowadays.'

Yes, a lot of work was the endless soaping and the trekking back and forth with cooking pots, always sooty, from the dining-room fire which was also called into service. 'Out of the way, out of the way,' Nana would shriek as she ran with a steaming pot through the narrow kitchen, down two steps and into the scullery, while we all pressed ourselves against the kitchen walls, feeling as though we had just witnessed the run of the Olympic torch. I remember too the heaving of buckets of copper-boiled water to the bathroom upstairs, through the kitchen, into the long hallway, up the stairs, over the landing, plonk into the bath and then downstairs for another. No need for cold water, it was lukewarm at the sixth bucketful. But God help you if the plug wasn't properly in and you lost the lot. She never asked us to help ('Can do it quicker myself') but baths were rationed in our house. Nana deserved something better than all that.

'You'll have to try the washer now you're here.'

'No, not for me. Can't bear machines, don't understand them.'

She had never had electricity. The years with my father, a warm and tolerant man, were lean ones. He couldn't afford to marry until he was nearly fifty and because there was no pension couldn't afford to retire from the editorship of his paper even in his seventies. However, in his last illness, still officially working at seventy-three, the firm did arrange for him a pension which was terminated by his death a week later. No part of it was passed on. It is not surprising that our house was never wired for electricity.

It is good to see Nana relaxing: in spite of her buoyancy her life has not been easy. Anne, a year or two younger than myself, had been born with a rare bone condition which showed itself in thin delicate joints moving awkwardly in their sockets, and in swollen wrists and knees. The doctors called it rickets, and later Perthe's disease, but it seems it was neither. My main memories are of Anne lying in a wheeled spinal chair, cheerful, but rigid in plaster from armpits to toes; of her running about awkwardly in a caliper splint, or again of her sipping red gravy from her father's spoon 'to build up her strength'. But later she was able to go to school on a tricycle and at eighteen had progressed enough to go to college. Except for a slight lameness, and the fact that any children she produced would be born by Caesarian section, Anne had apparently overcome her crippling condition and appeared to be quite normal. The long treatments over the years seemed to have paid off.

Unfortunately this was an illusion. The revelation came later after she had married Geoffrey Grant and had had her first child. The expected Caesarian caused no anxiety but Janet was born not only with her mother's handicaps but also with a cleft palate, very short sight and poor hearing. Four years later Penny was born with exactly the same disabilities.

As Geoff was serving in the Fleet Air Arm, Anne and her children made their home with Nana. No-one could guess what the future held for them.

† † †

Nana Loomes was powerful in adversity: it was then that she rose to her full potential. She had no self-pity in anything; she simply put her hand to the job and got on with it, cutting through problems like a plough through earth. That she did so with a certain amount of panache and argument was to her merely working up the adrenalin. After Janet's birth they realised that a backward drop of the head would be fatal, that she could not suck, and that she needed feeding every three hours, night and day, with a pipette, drop by patient drop. Because outside nursing was unobtainable Nana lit fires in bedrooms, helped with the night shift, cooked, washed, ran for the doctor and generally kept things going while Anne nursed the baby.

This continuing nightmare went on for about a year until the cleft palate was operated upon and Janet could feed normally. Then they were able to relax a little. When Penny was born with the same handicaps, the soft palate, not the hard, was found to be cleft and feeding was easier.

Anne never came to terms with the sorrow of her two handicapped children; to her they were an extension of herself. When Geoff was demobbed a few months later he and Anne bought a houseboat and went up with the children to a small harbour in Northumberland, near Newcastle, where Geoff had acquired a job, away from commiserating eyes and memories of heartbreak. Nana Loomes was alone again.

† † †

Among the treasures Nana brought with her this time was Anne's article on her houseboat, just published in 'The Nursery World'. I had heard very little from Anne since she and Geoff went to live on the boat. I had always thought of a houseboat as a simple adaptable one-roomed affair but this architect-designed one seemed in another category. Being no marine engineer I sneaked up to the little nursery to absorb all the details.

'It was not entirely the shortage of houses,' began the article, 'that brought about our decision to live in a houseboat. We had often discussed the possibilities of living afloat. Last year the chance arose. In Woodbridge, in Suffolk, after much searching, we finally saw Platters, a plain but solid conversion of Landing Craft Assault No. 62, forty feet long and ten feet wide. No engines - no cruising, an ideal boat for our purpose .. double diagonal built and all rooms lined with plywood, the ramp still down and in working order...

'The lay-out was simple. Through French windows you entered the saloon, heated by a coal stove, and from there a corridor ran the length of the boat to a double bedroom in the stern. Off the corridor was a pantry, bathroom, galley and what could be the children's bedroom. Ideal; all we needed was a berth, somewhere near my husband's work in the North...

'I joined Geoffrey to help search Northumberland for a mooring, but it was only after ten days of travel weariness, heartbreaks and arguments that we discovered it, in a storm, late evening, at the disused fishermen's harbour of Seaton Sluice, where the river joins the North Sea among rocks, flanked by

wonderful sands...

'To reach it, three months later, Platters had a journey of 350 miles from Suffolk by water, road and water again, and finally came to rest on a sandy shelf by a large sand dune. Here the local fishermen moored us permanently ready for the coming winter...

'The children love it. They don't fall overboard or catch colds. On the stern deck Janet plays with dolls and Penny the baby sleeps in the sun. Indeed Janet is out in all weathers and seems to have gained a proper sense of boat balance. At night we enjoy going to the dunes for ten minutes to watch the lights of the buoys, the lighthouses, the distant harbour of Blyth, and ships passing..

'Best of all we have discovered a flat grassy playground in a dip on the sand hill. High above the village, lying on your back in the sun, watching the clouds chase across the sky, you feel you are halfway to heaven. It will be wonderful in the summer. But even when the roar of the waves beyond the bar echoes up the valley and the fog signal persists forlornly, we know we are at the beginning of the life we have so long planned to live.'

February 27th

Glorious weather, with biting frost and brilliant sunshine and a jar of aconites on the table and I'm so tired that I don't care if I sit down and never get up again. The main cloud over the proceedings is the absence of Jeannie - four weeks now. At first it was very pleasant, peaceful and quiet, and I spent her wages each week, but now it is just hard work. Washing-up piles up alarmingly and so does dust. I shall be glad to see someone again or heaven knows how the baby will get clothed.

The children are working their way through a bout of coughs and colds. Roger has tonsillitis and earache and Nicola a chest cold. She is drooping around palely, and is past prescription - I'm told to see what develops next. I can't wait.

However, there may be light at the end of the tunnel. The Dr Barnardo hostel in the next road trains girls as mothers' helps, I hear. This could be an ideal solution, and to this end I have phoned the matron. She was a trifle vague about a suitable girl being free at the moment but sounded optimistic. So I am, as usual, keeping my fingers crossed.

March 20th

Well, well. Rita from Barnardo's is actually here, a fair, hefty pink and white girl like a country milkmaid, who adores Sue and has a sublime disregard for noise, thus adding to it on every occasion. She takes Sue out every afternoon and life is getting back to normal. I even have time to tack the stair carpet down.

Molly and Stewart McDougal have arrived in Flat 3, alongside us, so we have neighbours at last across the landing.

It is full spring this week, the rain having brought out myriads of bulbs. I feel detached and very fit, wondering if perhaps the baby isn't a dream and being surprised to find he/she is still there. Nicola now has progressed to flu; Roger's temperature is 103° and Nana has arrived for the birth. I don't think this well-thumbed exercise book will quite last. I shall have to start the Event with a new one.

† † †

April 11th

The Event is upon us.

A clear spring evening after a lovely day. Violets in the undergrowth, celandines on the banks; the family's clothes washed and ironed, the home-made Easter eggs finished and my bag packed. Seven o'clock. I take up the bag, it is time to go. A pity one cannot skip the next few hours. We go round the drive. Everything in the garden seems more than usually three-dimensional in the fading light. There's a tulip that will be out when I come back, and a yellow bush, kerria perhaps. The evening is quiet and warm, and there are sounds of Molly and Stewart on the landing behind. James and I hesitate whether to contact them, then decide to go and tell them after it's all over.

Across the wide road the lights are just beginning to twinkle. Here comes a number 90 bus, just when I have no need of it. We stand on the nursing home doorstep and ring the bell. A fresh young nurse opens the door and I say, with a bubble of merriment, 'I've come.' She looks just a little disconcerted and says, 'Did you phone?'

'No, I've walked over. We live opposite.'

She laughs. 'Oh well, come in,' and she takes the suitcase from James. 'Ring about ten, will you?' The door closes.

Ten o'clock.

The hours have ticked on, galloped on in a mad rush. In chaotic succession there come and go visions of white gloss paint, fluorescent lights, a little black mask with a funny little pipe, antiseptics and effort and pain. Strange how something that starts so intimately should end in this blaze of publicity.

Eleven o'clock. Only eleven? In a white room with chintzy curtains all is over. James comes in with a broad schoolboy grin, and Joanna is grizzling persistently in a cot, so soon. She is pink and gold like the others now she is washed, but what a sea-change from the slippery wet mass that slithered into the world an hour ago. Amazing how the mass becomes a little entity as soon as it cries. A lovely baby physically, they say, eight-and-a-quarter pounds and the process just the same as ever, but perhaps better organised owing to the little black mask.

April 13th

Today I've put on my ritzy bedjacket and am sitting among James's flowers, blue iris, pink tulips. I've addressed two dozen cards and am now prepared to be lazy. We're now dithering over the name; I'm not sure that I have the courage to go through with Joanna, which is outside the family tradition. Nevertheless it reminds me of someone tall, graceful and redhaired, and a bit out of the ordinary rut and I'm sure this little pink shrimp will be all of these; her hair already is reddish.

I suppose this is as near nirvana as I shall attain this side of the grave: a perfect spring day, flowers on the window-sill, immaculate surroundings, nurses to wait on me and nothing to do but relax and feed the baby. I've almost stopped thinking. Much of this is enforced: my pen has run out; I have read all the available books, received no letters, no visitors, children not being allowed and Nana Loomes having caught the flu. I'm living in a vacuum.

† † †

April 19th

Pain again, a world of pain, someone next door with pain for a bedfellow. Sardonic lover, pain. The only way to appease him is to give in to him. A nice little girl with a pleasant laugh ... 'It hasn't been so bad, so far. If it's a girl this time perhaps we'll have a boy next.' But that was last night, fifteen hours ago. Not all the frenzied phonings of her husband have helped one bit; they are parted by a bodyguard of white-clad nurses and a child that won't be born. Someone ought to have taught her to relax. Have we in some way thwarted the original plan of Nature? I suppose one day someone will care enough to make natural childbirth available to the masses. I'm afraid going into a huddle with Dr Dick Read's couple of books on the subject hasn't helped me very much, but it's a beginning. What one wants is a helper on the job who knows what's going on.

Well perhaps my daughter will benefit, but birth by relaxation will be too late for me.

April 23rd
Progress at last. A dear old medico, retired, acting as locum, came and talked to me today, light hand with a compliment, heavy with a prod, told me I looked younger than I really was and had done very well to have four children, very well. It all put up my morale no end and made me feel I could really cope in two days' time, when I know perfectly well I shan't.

Nana came across to see me at last at the weekend and shocked me utterly, a pale shadow of the warrior I really knew. The flu she caught from Nicola had paled her and thinned her down, and for once she looked seventy-two. But on her second visit last night she was more like herself, told me in detail of the sheep's head pie she had made James: 'I simmered it for three hours, let it get cold, took the meat off the bone and popped it in the big green pie-dish with a crust on. Delicious!' and about the groceries that didn't arrive: 'I told them I wanted them specially for Tuesday but that man behind the counter must be half-daft because by tea-time they hadn't come, so I had to go down to the kiosk and telephone, and I can't BEAR telephoning. However ...' and off she goes at a tangent to give me up-to-date news of Royalty's latest goings-on. Royalty is meat and drink to Nana Loomes. If you chaff her, she'll say: 'My dear, I saw Queen Victoria driving to her Jubilee in 1897,' as if that capped the matter and for most people it does. To bring us both down to earth I gave her a shopping list to prepare for my return tomorrow and she departed with a purpose in life again.

☦   ☦   ☦

25

May 1st

The lotos-eating had to end and I've been home a week.

A wonderful May Day, clear and sunny, Joanna's christening day, and she is three weeks old. We have finally compromised with Shakespeare and Rosalind is to be her second name; and I am established with her in the little playroom over the garden. She snuffles softly beside me in the wicker cot.

These are the days before the outside world breaks in. Now I have time to write, and read a little; and get to know Joanna, she and I growing to strength together.

So too is the garden, each day producing some new plant in the undergrowth. So far we've found blue borage, bluebells and greater celandine in profusion, and there is a blackbird's nest in the yew hedge and the newt pond is full of greeny-yallery little straddlers transfixed by rays of sunshine. James declares he saw a heron yesterday gazing speculatively into the pond, so maybe that's goodbye to the newts.

May 15th

Values seem a bit muddled these days, to say nothing of routine. I still hang on from day to day cabbagely happy in the sparkling weather and putting off the moment of real coping. But it must come. Nicola has had her seventh birthday (without a cake) and Nana has had to return home. And Sue has 'Reet' from Barnardo's round her little finger. I marvel again at Sue's colouring under the bronze-red hair, I who ought to be used to it, and at the intelligence behind it all, so now and again I start some blank verse:

> Warm as a peach against a sunny wall,
> Peach rare, peach beautiful ...

or: The tiny amber riot of her hair ...

but the Muse doesn't last.

May 30th

The coping has begun.

Yesterday Nicola walked in her first procession at Church, all dressed up in the dress I had made, with much sweat, from a nylon parachute, and with her pigtails sticking out behind. I looked for her with some excitement in the train of little girls all dressed alike, and at first glance missed her altogether through looking among the bigger ones. Second time round I found her, pale-faced, big-eyed, not at all the tempestuous person of home. She enjoyed the procession, probably because of wearing the wreath and veil as much as for the religious side, but it had been an Experience, something to be notched up. We walked home together in the bitter spring evening, she eager with her thin legs and short skirt and school hat, chattering like a magpie.

She had said to Molly McDougal, who always tells the children she's twenty-one, 'Well my Mummy's thirty-six so if you're twenty-one she looks younger than you do.' I see apologies ahead.

Roger at five is a philosopher. I had said, 'I don't know why children must always be doing something they oughtn't; it's such a struggle,' and he retorted, 'Well, you *have* little girls and boys; you must put up with them.'

June

Here we go: Roger and Nicola have mumps. His is the biggest face I've seen.

July

Sue now has mumps too but is a plucky little patient. She has a large pale face and is rather quiet. Nicola on the other hand has a small pale face and is very crotchety. The weather is superb and one ought to be lying out in it, but one isn't. Tonight instead I have been making strawberry jam and bottling, and as I only get three pounds of jam for my trouble it turns out expensive. The mumpers called down continously and testily until the lights were lit, nearly ten o'clock. James, needing release of spirit, went for a cycle ride.

In all this, three-month-old Joanna gurgles peacefully and no-one has time to notice if she doesn't. At present we're having to keep her apart from Sue. 'Baby catch my fat face,' says Sue sorrowfully. The mumpers progress slowly, and instead of signing off Roger, the doctor gave me a note for the aural surgeon at the hospital, which made me reflect somewhat savagely that bringing up four youngsters would be nothing if they could just remain well for a decent period.

Rita from Barnardo's, who should be my prop and support in such crises, is as scatty as they make them. I sent her out for half a pound of coffee and a pound and a half of fruit. She lost the shopping list, spent ten minutes looking for it, forgot to take a basket, bought one pound of fruit and one and a half pounds of coffee, and came home with them all in her arms. Once I found her scouring Nana's silver with a pot scourer and one dinner-time she burnt the peas and potatoes and forgot to cook the sausage at all, so we had eggs for dinner.

October

Once out of the doldrums of mumps, coughs, colds and flu the children reveal some interesting traits. Sue's vocabulary is increasing. 'I'll go shopping tomorrowday,' she says, 'with Joanna my sister'. She talks of her 'jama tot and the tea tot (all pots and tops are tots to her) and the sykepedia has entered her life. So have 'Christians' (crisps) and 'ice keen' and 'totos' (taters). We might say Sue now almost speaks the English language.

Roger and Nicola argue, fiercely.

'Joanna's a girl.'

'Joanna's a boy.'

'Anyway,' says Roger, 'you don't know what she'll be till she grows up.'

Nicola squirms. 'I know something better than that.'

'What?'

'I know a man who died and left twelve children, all of them babies.'

Roger didn't know enough to refute this so he said sourly, 'He'd have to lay a lot of eggs to get twelve babies.'

He is very much aware of female bodies, particularly grown-up ones, and hugged an aunt who came unexpectedly, with the exclamation, 'Aren't you goreously *fat*, Auntie Doris!' so that she didn't know whether to be riled or flattered. He followed that up, when we were talking about Christmas presents, by shouting suddenly with an expansive movement across his chest, 'I know what I'll make Nana Barnard this year, a brassiere, 'cos that's what she wants.' Wants or needs, I wondered, in the dead silence that followed this outburst, but he'd got the word right, must have been quietly researching it.

‡   ‡   ‡

In fact one of the joys of being in Norwich is that we are near James's mother, at Lowestoft. Nana Barnard is the ideal materfamilias, a warm,

28

plump, maternal figure who rules the clan with a loving despotism and a twinkle in her eye. There is a timeless earthy quality about her that is allied to a great tolerance and sense of fun. Yet, if in watching her you thought that here was only a smiling matriarch, you'd be wrong, for Nana B., tho' she can be impish, is downright and dead practical. Below the laughter wrinkles around that tolerant mouth you suddenly find a very strong chin, jutting out firmly just when you think the pleasant face is rounding off. Nana B. will bide her time but she won't be beaten.

It was a revelation to me to know her, brought up as I was in a commonsense, 'little-girls-should-be-seen-and-not-heard' sort of household. I had never met anyone quite so open-hearted. In all the years that she was head of a large family with five children of her own and one of her sister's, the door was always open. People just came and stayed, or came all day and went home only to sleep, or came with their families after years away with not so much as by-your-leave. Yet even when she lived in the depths of the country I've never known her beat for supplies and when she saw a cavalcade of visitors coming up the path she'd screw up her eyes just long enough to identify them and then pop into the Aga some five-minute bread, or disappear into the pantry with a bowl and with a cake ready for the oven. Nana never fussed and she kept her own counsel. If you'd just walked in from Australia (and some did that) not a hair on her head would stir.

People came to Meadowfield to recover from operations, broken engagements and shaky finances. There was a healing quality about Nana B.

When I was first married and going back and forth from table to kitchen forgetting things, she used to say, 'Let your head save your feet,' and when I was having spasms of conscience over a decision (which was often) she would say with a wicked grin, 'Do what *you* want. If you've pleased yourself you've pleased somebody,' a distilled drop of the truth if ever there was one.

One of the healing qualities of Nana B. is that there is no competitiveness in her, no keeping-up with the Joneses. She makes you feel that you do everything better than she does and yet never is this true, except perhaps for a slight eccentricity in writing letters. She writes only when there is no other way of communicating, to say that she is coming over on the diesel Tuesday and bringing a cooked chicken, or to wish James a happy birthday and cake on the way. These sporadic notes, written on anything that comes to hand, like the back of a bill, are by us more preciously preserved than manuscripts. One written on the back of a hardware account, slanted at 35 degrees and rather breathless, finished up: 'Sorry no more, dear boy, I am in a terrible.' Ever since then it is accepted that if we hear nothing from Nana Barnard she is in a terrible.

✝   ✝   ✝

November 5th

Guy Fawkes night and the weather has broken. It rained so much we let off the fireworks in the porch with five squealing children dancing round - including two Robertsons from downstairs.

Three of the five, our three, have only just gone to bed and have been saying prayers. I said, 'God bless you all,' and Sue echoed, 'God bress doo all,' and everybody laughed. But I feel a chill tonight. The summer is just a memory and the gales are rising. Under the trees everything is sodden.

November 6th

James had a disturbing phone call at the office from Nana this morning to say that Anne had been taken to hospital with some unspecified illness and she was going north immediately. Cold and uneasy I went to bed early, filled with a sense of foreboding.

November 7th

Dear God, a foreboding indeed. Anne died at ten o'clock this morning in the ambulance on the way to Tynemouth hospital. She was thirty-four. Thirty-four! What can have happened? I find it utterly chilling that Anne should be lying there on the slab of a hospital in the north while no doubt the two young children play around oblivious on the boat. The telegram said, 'Pneumonia and heart failure.' I can't connect either of these with Anne, she never had a weak heart; she was never prone to chest trouble. Other things, but not those. There is something unusual here. Why so suddenly? Did she know she was so ill? And what on earth was yesterday like for them all when Geoff phoned if she died this morning? The questions have pounded into my head like drumbeats all during this desolate day.

They were going to do so much, Anne and Geoff; their life together had only just begun. Anne was going to write, they were going to pay off the boat and make up for the years apart. Tomorrow and tomorrow... But there is no tomorrow, no tomorrow at all. Life is here and now, you take it or you lose it, and it never slipped by two people so cruelly. They had their blissful year and it is ended; there will be no more Anne Grant however long the world lasts.

Hold on to this last vibration of warmth: it will become stone cold as the days go on. Today she is still Anne: tomorrow she will be a memory.

† † †

November 10th

There has been a post-mortem. Anne died of meningitis. From the first crippling symptoms it only ran a course of four or five days. Knowing what it can do to people I can't help feeling it was better for her to go.

Nana had gone north at the first alarum and Geoff met her with the news at the station. I was afraid the whole business might overwhelm her but today she sent a brisk practical letter and made us feel better. Trust in the Lord,' said she, 'and it'll clear.'

The turn of the knife comes in all this funeral ritual. I ordered flowers by phone. We talked of 'it' and 'she', and the coffin, of anything but Anne Grant. Such phrases are the veil over the emotions, the barrier against heartbreak. Gradually - though, thank God, not completely yet - she is being turned into the dear departed.

Anne is being buried on Saturday in a cemetery at the edge of the sea overlooking St. Mary's Island. It strikes a chill in me to think of her remains being left there on the grey windy coast, miles from us all. I know how unsympathetic the north-east coast can be in the storms and the winter. It doesn't alter my ultimate faith but I should like to think of her last resting-place as somewhere soft and verdant. When my time comes I hope they bury me near a green meadow where buttercups come in spring and there are trees.

James says he doesn't mind a tinker's cuss where his body goes as long as his soul's in the right place. Perhaps; but the sense of personal immortality affects me strongly. The way people are buried or destroyed reflects the way they lived or what they stood for: a grave forgotten is a person forgotten.

31

The question now arises of what Geoff, alone in a houseboat, will do with the children. Janet is five, Penny twenty months and not yet walking. He can't employ anyone to live in because there are no completely separate bedrooms. It looks as if they may have to leave Platters. As a temporary measure, until he could sell the boat and get a house (and who is going to buy a houseboat in Northumberland?), he suggests they might go to the Sisters of Nazareth in Newcastle or to his relations, or almost certainly to Nana Loomes. But what of the permanent solution? James and I sat up late talking about it.

In our hearts I think we always knew the answer; it was just a matter of clearing away the practical difficulties. James and I are of one mind that if Geoff is willing we will take the two little ones with our children until something turns up. James will be going north for the funeral and can discuss it with both sides of the family.

But there's no doubt now we would have to find another house, no doubt at all.

November 18th

In a single week it has turned to near-winter. The trees, still green when James went up for the funeral, are flaring flame and yellow. Last night the gales came again; they hurtle now across the garden and through the attic cracks.

A grim week, both here and in the north. By the Sunday after Anne's death I had developed a toxic condition from a gnatbite in the leg, and was feeling rather sorry for myself, but Nana Barnard as usual turned up trumps and came over, bringing with her a wild duck and a huge fruit cake. Whether it was the cheering presence of Nana or the wild duck I don't know, but my palpitations have gradually disappeared and I've come to the conclusion that the house runs better without me now I'm laid up. Remote control, firm and applied frequently as James does it, is probably better for Rita.

November 30th

The result of the family deliberations is that we take the children. I think Geoff's sister-in-law would have liked to have taken one of them as she has no family of her own, but as there are probably years of medical supervision ahead it was thought better to keep them together and have them treated together. They will have each other, and they can continue being brought up in their mother's faith as Catholics, with which Geoff is in agreement.

So with the leg healing slowly we've been to look at several houses and this is where Eaton End comes into the diary because of all of them it is the one that appeals to us most. The house and garden cover almost an acre and it has a small orchard of apple trees. It is situated up round the bend of the next long road from here, where the small houses give way to solid family ones on the edge of Eaton village; it is semi-detached, Edwardian, and goes up to three storeys, but one of its joys, even seen through a November drizzle, is the large garden stretching out on one side. The house would seem to suit us too; there have been three large boys in it for eleven years and the odd banister is out and the odd window broken. There are also seven bedrooms, the top ones up in the trees again, which has a great appeal for me.

December 2nd

We have thrown our cap over the windmill. James has bought Eaton End at a public auction for an amount which of course we don't possess, but he is going to suggest that Nana Loomes should sell her old house and come in with us, physically and financially. As this arrangement is still quite nebulous we sat last night like two glum crows either side of the fireplace doing accounts. It seems more than likely that there is a cheese-paring future in front of us again just when we thought we were emerging, but on the other hand Eaton End is a fine proposition, large, well-worn, and full of possibilities, just like us.

† † †

Eaton End
January 16th 1950

Sue's third birthday and we're into Eaton End, measles and all. Three of the children being covered with spots, and taxis really being taboo, Bill Robertson came to the rescue with his car. With the youngsters wrapped up in rugs we transferred them from bare boards at Fernlea to bare boards at Eaton. I supervised arrangements walking on a stick and the insurance man who had popped in also helped us to move the furniture. As I've said before, we've never yet moved in normal fashion, the way other people do, but this was fairly painless and the three eldest children being safely incarcerated we had a free hand. There have been small snags of course. The contents of the dining-room have been changed round three times already and we have tried to wipe out the on-going chocolate paint with a shade known on the charts as 'stone', an everlasting job-to-be rather like painting the Forth Bridge, I imagine.

We straightened up the kitchen first and the battleship lino went in beautifully, but we found that every floor in the house had had a different lino and some had several on top of each other, so that the one-colour flowing effect so dear to ideal home magazines is missing at Eaton, and the peacock blue of the first floor reappears in odd places, notably in the top floor attic.

But considering that we are trying to make seven bedrooms out of what were store-rooms and boxrooms we are not doing too badly. We have left two big rooms, Nana's and the nieces', empty until after the sale hoping that some of Nana's furniture may turn up. The main aim is to have a reasonably straight house for them to come into and we are just hoping that Nana can cope until this happens. Already Janet and Penny have moved down to Peterborough with her and time presses somewhat.

But I'm afraid this isn't a very good way to convalesce.

January 26th

Oh what a change from the optimism of home. Here I crawl back from the Midlands, grey-faced and full of cold after a nightmare four days, wondering in a detached kind of way if I shall ever have a lighthearted household again. The set-up in Peterborough was grim and confused, and really ought never to have been allowed to happen. Nana has the almost impossible task of making the children feel at home and at the same time

34

of preparing the house for sale next month. She has been there forty years and the encrustations of a lifetime have piled up in it. Coping with the kiddies as well is beyond her. Both of them have crashing colds which run unchecked, and Penny has a malformation due to the cleft palate which causes all her food to liquidise and return down her nose too. She cries perpetually in the strange surroundings and though she is not articulate at twenty months, she doubtless knows that her mother is just not there. After lunch and at night Nana goes up and lies beside her to 'sleep her in', a small comfort in an alien world, but for Nana time-consuming.

For the first two days Penny's sombre brown eyes, like melancholy prunes, followed me round unblinkingly, without recognition. I was just one of the many new faces she had seen in the last month. In many ways Penny is self-sufficient. Though she can stand but not walk, she can dress herself, feed herself and support herself at a chair and play with tiny things. But she makes no attempt to move from the position in which one left her, either by crawling nor by hitching herself along. Thinking over this objectively, I think she is physically unable to do either, as lack of movement in the joints is part of the bone deficiency. As a result of this inaction, if she wants anything she cries. Penny finds the present world hostile and who can blame her? Yet on the last day she began to know me and to melt a little and left to ourselves we got on quite well.

Janet, on the other hand, is a lively child and is longing to come to Norwich to Auntie Mary's, even though being in Nana's house was like coming home again and the surroundings were reassuring. Outwardly Janet looks like a little fairy, a waif. She has delicate marble-white colouring with pale finespun hair and enormous blue eyes, blurred with thick glasses, which are her lifeline. Janet is almost blind without them and in the early years before anyone realised this she constantly fell over things without putting out her hand to save herself. She used to fall quite flat and she still has a permanent bump on her forehead as a legacy of it. Her cleft palate has been expertly repaired, the only evidence being a slight thickening of her speech; there are no outside scars with either child. Janet's limbs are delicate, brittle, with enlarged wrist and ankle joints, but underneath all her apparent disabilities she appears to be fairly tough. She does not give up easily and has a lively curiosity. Nature, it seems, works out its compensations.

On the fourth day I decided to bring the youngsters back to Eaton earlier than I had planned. It seems more important that we get them settled in permanent surroundings with the other children than that we should wait until we are respectably curtained and decorated.

February 2nd

So here we are all together at last, Janet, Penny, Sue, Joanna, Roger, Nicola and, of course, Rita. The family complete except for Nana Loomes. Sue, three, took Janet, five, in her brown buttoned boots, and off they went to explore the secret places: Joanna and Penny sat and explored each other, chattering the while. Everything went very smoothly at first, probably because Nana Barnard popped over yet again to help with the settling-in. After she left, things became involved.

The nieces brought their streaming colds with them: we all caught them. Sue developed earache and Joanna coughed a tight little cough and cried with it. James thought Nicola might have pleurisy and Sue was found to have inflammation of the ear. On one of the blackest days I woke up with leaden limbs to find Joanna already crying and by afternoon she was very distressed. I lit a steam kettle and sat by the gas fire with her for a while. How many years, I thought sitting there, have I spent in the dimmed nursery light to the smell of camphorated oil and the sound of difficult breathing, and how many more years to come? It is part of the pattern of childhood: cough mixture, camphorated oil, fretfulness, night lights; perspiration beading pink-and-white complexions, sturdy bodies thrashing restlessly, inhalant, aspirin, Mummy, Mummy...And now quite suddenly the pattern changing to sombre dark eyes, tiny brittle limbs, dead white faces. No Mummy.

It would have helped if I could have leaned on Rita, but she was quite oblivious to it all. One afternoon she went out for medicine and ear-drops, taking with her Roger and Janet for some fresh air. They returned minus medicine or drops, hugging several bags of potato crisps.Couldn't find the chemist's. As the medicine was essential I got up from my tea and fetched them myself. I stood at the bus stop wondering whether anyone outside a concentration camp had ever felt so tired, since I had been up half the night and slept only near dawn. How pleasant to die and leave it all! But it is always Mum who wakes up first with that kind of sixth sense. One gets sorry for oneself in extreme fatigue and I am reflecting soberly, bussing back with the bottles and ear-drops clutched to my shrinking bosom, that I should have had my tea and made Rita go back to find the chemist's.

However we all have our limits and one lunch-time, after pushing Rita all the morning and finding her still dreaming over the washtub while I prepared dinner, I went on strike. I walked out and left her to dish up. I took my bike and went out in the cold sunshine for an hour and by the time I returned it was to a very sober kitchen. James was home and Rita in subdued fashion was dishing up. I gathered she had received a few home truths.

February 11th

Nevertheless we have worked our way through the first days together, somehow. Two of the children have got back to school in bitter winds and rain, and each day is a day nearer to spring and good weather. Little by little, the coughs have subsided, the temperatures have abated, the adjustments have been made. We are still finding out all the small psychological quirks that must accompany an upheaval like ours; that Penny for instance tears everything tearable into tiny pieces, is not yet potty-trained, is addicted to eating earth, with the result that the mud comes down her nose and all over her face. This will adjust itself in time, they say. Janet regularly empties out her suitcase just for the joy of counting her belongings; is very possessive and quite ready to elbow Sue out of the way ('Her can't play'), which, while showing she is quite at home, is a great test of our impartiality. We found too that Rita was quite ready to sit down with the lot of them and play games at any hour of the day, but to work, never.

To round off the whole sorry tale Rita has now gone to bed, top attic, with what we think is bronchitis and the doctor says he'll come back in a week!

Coming downstairs one day after ministering to Rita, I found a trail of soap flakes on each step and along the hall.

'What's this for?' I yelled to all and sundry.

Nicola poked a worried face round the banister post.

'That's my trail. That's so's I can find my way back in the jungle.'

Jungle! That's just about it.

╪   ╪   ╪

37

Survival

With the first crocuses came Nana Loomes. She sailed up in a taxi, in a new hat with a mauve ostrich feather, exuding energy in such proportions that for all her spare frame she seemed to be twice as large as life.

'Train was late,' she announced, kissing us all abstractedly. 'How do you like my feather? Nelly Harrison's, remember? She wore it at Tom's funeral. I thought it went well with the coat. A lady in the train leaned over to me and said, "Excuse me commenting, but you do look elegant."'

She broke off for a moment to pay the taximan, admonishing him to mind the trunk (Grandma's) as it wouldn't stand much handling, and not to forget the cases and particularly the cardboard box, and then stood amid the mêlée, vigorous, alert, pouring out with exasperation the tale of the sale of the house. The night before it took place apparently, the cistern in the bathroom burst and the water cascaded down the stairs. So she sent for Wade the plumber, aptly named, and told him to come immediately.

'He wanted to know what I was worrying about, the customers had all been to view it anyway, and I was just to turn the water off and he'd be round when he could.'

But the thing that rankled most about her uprooting was the fact that the movers had packed a whole heap of the wrong stuff in among the right.

'Fancy! My back was turned for half-an-hour and what did they do? They picked up the whole kitchen-table full of rubbish and packed the lot. Rotten lot of stuff. You need eyes in the back of your head these days.'

I'm afraid she had always needed them in the back of her head. Nana was always being caught out by happenings over which she felt she should have had control. Events simply plotted against her, lay in wait and pounced. She was therefore constantly pitting herself against such eventualities in advance.

But apart from the rubbish that came accidentally I can see that Nana's Victorian furniture, however we may decry it, is going to furnish the rest

38

of the house. Already a bow-fronted chest of drawers has swallowed up Janet's precious belongings and two others will soon be filled with Roger's and Sue's. Delicate bedroom chairs with straw seats appear in odd places around the house and we are picking our way through what-nots and overmantels and mentally stripping them down.

We have put Nana in the large back bedroom at the top of the first stairs, overlooking the garden and the long drive that winds down to the empty garage. She is in a strategic position here for the nieces in the bedroom next door, for the bathroom and the stairs; in fact for everything on this floor including our own bedroom. The facilities of the bathroom she has, however, already dismissed. 'I'll use it for washing of course, but I've got my own pot under the bed.'

Her bedsitting-room is taking shape round her vast sideboard, a bureau and a large coloured picture of a lady with a hound entitled 'Anxious Hearts'. The lady is sitting, looking out wistfully through a mullioned window, with her arm resting on a huge retriever. I like 'Anxious Hearts'. It has an element of romance about it and the lady is wearing a fichu, a favourite confection of mine. The sideboard, dating back to the period of Art Nouveau, when Nana married William Pettit, is embellished with beaten copper panels of stylised tulips and much intricate carving and has the advantage of being commodious. Into this has gone her crockery and Limoges china, her silver épergne, her canteen of cutlery and Japanese bronzes; her bezique set and my father's chess pieces, and her knitting needles and patterns.

The wine compartment with its separate bottle-sized divisions is stuffed with underwear, tins of buttons and biscuits; with mending pieces ('Can't throw those away, they'll come in useful somewhere, James' pyjamas I should think'); with Great-Aunt Jane's black fox collar and several of Nana's gaily coloured hats, for Nana loves hats.

But not quite all is confined to the sideboard and bureau. There is also Grandma's trunk, a domed black shiny wicker affair that completely absorbs all the bedlinen and Edwardiana. To me as a child rummaging in this trunk was an adventure and to my children it will be a treasure box. If you dive to the bottom you will find curled feathers, purple and black, bodices sewn with jet, a hand-quilted négligé; a paste buckle set with amethysts and a Limerick lace collar. There is also a blue velvet corsage, of a singing blue not seen nowadays, shaped and boned ready to fit over a bustled skirt.

None of this is new to me: I could tell you the contents of Grandma's trunk by heart. But it will be new to the youngsters if they are allowed anywhere near it.

Rita meanwhile has housemaid's knee and has been out of action for a week. I installed her in the kitchen, leg up, sitting pretty, while we did all the work around her.

† † †

Now and again there are compensations. Stewart MacDougal from the flat took me out to a country hospital to see Molly who has had an operation. It was a cold brilliant sunny day, the countryside clean and clear as if it had been spring-cleaned after the winter, stark and exceptionally three-dimensional. Elms stood etched against the far woods, green shoots against furrows, racing clouds against the blue sky. Pleasant drive through Wymondham with its old market cross and timbered houses. Pleasant hour with Molly lapped in the warmth of central heating, with gentle chatter about operations and jumpers and oranges, with me taking in the surroundings with special care because I might find myself here one day. Then back into the knife-like wind and fading day to the chores at home.

April 10th
The long winter seems over, the buds are bursting, the myrabella plum blossom frothing, and today has been like summer instead of the usual stingy windiness of Norfolk in spring. It will be fun watching what comes up in the garden, though at present I'm pretty busy watching what develops inside. Rita is now in bed again, three storeys up, with stiff neck and earache, all meals taken up. The doctor prescribed a week in bed, said he would return and has not been seen since.

April 14th
In spite of the mêlée inside the house, the garden grows to beauty. It is charming this sunny April morning. Under the walnut tree there are wallflowers; daffodils line the big border; seedboxes litter the vinery and the pink peach blossom is out on the south-west wall. I've had flu and Geoffrey is coming down on a coaling boat from Newcastle for Easter. I hope he sees a difference in his youngsters. Penny has beaten even Joanna

40

for rapid development; she walks firmly, talks more, plays more energetically, is fatter and looks more cheerful. Joanna is coming along nicely too: at one year she climbed stairs and then, affrighted, looked back at the precipice. I see her prowess growing daily. Yesterday she ate three raw eggs and a pot of paint water and today had a go at the chickens' balancer meal. It rained in the late morning and she scooped up the mud in various little cavities and utensils and ate it. Three times I washed her face free of mud, something I usually do for Penny. 'Why bother?' said Roger when I complained, 'Mud's wonderful for the face.'

At present she lunges bandily around in laboured circles. A little run precipitates a fall and then the slow lunging process begins all over again. Like a Churchill tank she is, but with both elbows up and out. She also purloins jam tarts off the trolley, picks pieces off the joint and plunges both hands into paint and eats that. Her taste is impartial. She and Penny are like Laurel and Hardy: Joanna fat, bandy and convoluted; Penny thin, bolt upright and with tiny feet turned out.

We missed Joanna one morning. 'Spect she's gone out of the gate,' says Sue nonchalantly. But no, the huge gate was still on the latch; we found her in her usual place round by the front door. She was sitting quite still beside a dying bird. It lay on the gravel and twitched a little. We took it round to the kitchen and tried to revive it with warm milk, lacking any brandy, but it died very soon.

'It's dead,' said Roger.

Joanna was upset. 'Deaded,' she echoed in great agitation.

The children buried it in one of the low hollow pillars edging the drive, they being child-sized and receptacles of everything unattached, like marbles, apple cores and small toys. In the evening when the little ones were asleep Roger dug it up 'to see what it looked like', but not being very impressed he reburied it.

'I s'pose dead birds are like dead people,' he remarked philosophically, 'not much fun with no life in them.'

41

April 2nd 1950

It is now three months since we moved here, and I think I might say we're settling in at Eaton End, though whether we're settling *down* is another matter. We are rather like ill-shaped cobbles jostling for position in the family terrain. It reminds me of my father quoting old Macadam of tarmacadam fame who said that stones of unequal size and shape will never settle in the surface of the road because one pushes the other out and I reckon this is exactly what is happening to us. Already some of the squarer ones are being chipped off at the corners (depending on the degree of granite therein), but surprisingly it's not the children who need to adjust to each other. They are happy as Larry. It's the grownups.

From the start my efforts to draft a timetable for the three of us in the kitchen have failed miserably. I make a weekly list, stuck clearly on the kitchen wall, of jobs to be done and the days in which to do them. Nana does exactly the opposite and Rita does nothing at all. If I've written 'Mum wash whites' Nana comes down with an armful of woollies and competes for the sink. When the list says 'Rita; clean and polish kitchen floor', an ironing board and pile of linen appear in the middle of it, and there is much to-do with Nana about damping, folding, airing, taking most of the morning, while the floor remains dirty. If I scrawl 'Sheets out Monday' I get a dollop out Friday. I reason, I expostulate, but it is words on the wind.

James, who is good with a cliché, says, 'What did you expect anyway? You can't put a young head on old shoulders nor an old head on young ones. Be patient, it will sort itself out.' But I can't be patient, nor can I muddle along, and in three months I think the pattern is firmly set. I've come to the conclusion that, willing as Nana is, we are both operating in separate orbits, meeting only to clash. Nana has been used to running her household and I mine.

Nevertheless we have fallen into a fairly regular routine. Every day I put out a line twenty yards long of mixed washing, mostly nappies, Penny's quota added to Joanna's making a rare display. Quite often the line breaks with the extended weight and we wrench yet another prop from the shrubbery trees. The one commodity we are really short of, apart from money, is bedclothes, the nieces not having brought any from the boat and Nana's being fifty years old and paper thin. But where there is any life in a blanket or sheet Nana will stretch it further by turning it sides to middle and joining it up again. She is the best sides-tomiddler I've ever come across. And if she likes cutting and joining-up I like re-covering, so we dump the old eiderdowns in my huge washer, drying them in the fine spring weather and I painstakingly cover them with fresh cottons. To outsiders this may seem a chore but to me a new eiderdown wrenched from obscurity is as satisfying as any other form of art. However all these things are time-consuming and there is just no time, no time at all. The days whizz by.

May 31st

I've always known we had a Pioneer in the family but it seems that fame has caught up with her at last. And indeed fortune if you can call it that. Nana Loomes has been back to her home town for a presentation. It all went back to 1902, when in her early twenties she became headmistress of the new local infants' school, and was followed after her second marriage by her founding, with my father, the Fletton Infant Welfare Centre in 1917. In 1922 she became one of the early women magistrates and shortly afterwards a governor of the secondary school. Now that she has left Peterborough for good, all the folk she worked with over the years subscribed to a cheque: the parents whom she taught all those years ago and their children and grandchildren; the mothers she ministered to at the Welfare Centre and their children; ex-colleagues of the Petty Sessional Court, fellow-governors of the secondary school, and members of the Nursing Association of which she was eventually organiser. A formidable array.

We had a rehearsal for the Great Day and in the end Nana wore her black hat with purple ostrich feather, her astrakhan coat and her buckled shoes and looked every inch a duchess. In Peterborough Town Hall she made a modest but totally relevant speech, the first she had ever made in her life, and had a fine photograph in the local press making it. My father would have been very proud of her. We were.

Nana's cheque was for two hundred and sixty pounds and she returned in a warm and rosy glow which took some days to dispel. A pity, I thought, watching her animated face and listening to her lively comments, that it should ever fade, for there would be quite enough nappy-washing and nose-blowing in the future. But we had a heartwarming hour reading through the letters which had come with the donations. Then they were carefully tied up with white tape, labelled 'Letters re presentation' and put away in the bureau.

The Welfare Centre itself had been built on the proceeds of Buttercup Flag Days and the enamelled key of the Centre was engraved with a buttercup. This too was gently laid in its case and put away.

'Might be history one day,' said Nana. 'Someone might write about it, you never know.' In diaries, for instance.

Then she was able to turn her attention to the spending of the cheque. The man from the Pensions Office told her that to qualify for her twenty-six shillings weekly she must dispose of about £90 capital. So off she went on a spree.

First she bought a pearl necklace to go with her crimson woollen dress for when she had people to tea. Then she invested in a large green carpet for her room and some flowered curtains to go with it, stopping off on the way to buy me a dress. And most important of all she chose some new clothes for the nieces, perhaps to replace the patched liberty bodices and buttoned boots.

She came home in a taxi surrounded by these parcels as pleased as Punch, and her last flutter was to give James a sizeable cheque towards a solid fuel stove in the kitchen. By the weekend she reckoned she'd knocked off the requisite ninety pounds and could meet the pension man with a clear conscience.

'Never had such a spree in my life,' she said gleefully. It never ocurred to her to go off and spend it on herself, having a holiday.

'Might as well have it where you can see it and enjoy it,' she declared, busily machining rufflette tapes on the curtains, 'and a stove will be here years after I've gone.' True, though only the generous would see it that way.

June 1950

We are now tackling Eaton End. Among the dandelions and daisies the tennis court looks like being mown at last. There have been setbacks. First the secondhand mower failed to work; then the equally ancient net was put up and we found the rats had eaten a hole in it, and finally, when it was pulled nice and taut, poor short-sighted Janet ran into it and snapped the wire. Now James and company are looking for last year's corners: there are two metal ones, we were told, which always become overgrown in winter. The helpers all take bearings from these, which they are sure will lead to the others, but of course do not, for though the whole family walks up and down in the proper direction for half an hour they

44

cannot find the limey-white right-angles where the grass was marked last summer.

Ah! here comes Janet puffing upstairs for the measuring-tape. They have found the third and fourth corners and all is well. We stop and celebrate with orange squash, rather like the roof-topping ceremony in Bavaria. Something of this kind is always being celebrated in our family; I think because answers to problems are seen to be some sort of miracle rather than the result of organisation. There is now a fifty-fifty chance of getting the court ready for the office party in ten days' time. The motive is strong. James will be showing off his new estate to his colleagues. We've even finished decorating the dining-room, where the players will be changing. It is now painted a soft peach due to James' and Rita's efforts, and the carpet, shampooed by three of us and well tramped on by Joanna, looks like velvet.

June 10th

On the evening of the party we put up our assorted deckchairs along the touchline, together with an ancient metal garden seat brought here by Nana which is at least as old as I am and more drunken-looking, covered it with rugs, and it looked quite inviting. I arranged lemonade and biscuits in the kitchen and put the four youngest to bed early. By the time I'd done this and changed into tennis things I hadn't much driving power left, let alone tactics. We had discovered a few home truths about our tennis patch when practising for the great day. The sides of the court are completely open and the spectators are therefore excellent targets for bad shots, and as you rootle for balls among the potato rows, the loganberries alongside them, all-clawing, take the T-shirt off your back. Indeed the gooseberries aren't much better (my children will never believe babies were born under gooseberry bushes), and it is past belief how many guises a lost tennis ball will take on, the colour of stones, apples, or turds, or else it just remains greeny-brown under a tuft of grass defying us all.

The office staff, however, oblivious of such niceties, arrived by bike and car down the drive and it was obvious from the moment their feet touched grass that the general spirit was willing though the tactics were individually weak. Everyone except James's efficient secretary was a bit wobbly on the serve or slow to the net, and we were no examples ourselves. It is surprising how human traits show up on a tennis court: your domineering know-all smashes his ball aggressively but blindly into the net, whereas your meticulous clerk from the rating section nips back and forth on the baseline and returns all the shots his boss has missed. Yes, by and large I enjoyed the tennis party.

Halfway through it Nicola and Roger carefully brought out the lemonade and biscuits and then as the evening became chill we left the hardiest four to finish their set and went into the house for coffee. I think this was for me the pleasantest part of the affair.
We all sat and mardled and became quite cosy
and someone started to boast a little and
someone else told Norfolk stories. And then
at last one of the party thought he ought to
be getting back to his wife and he
reluctantly set off the exodus.

Ringside seat

June 19th

A superb fortnight of clear skies broken by occasional deluges; dappled shade, warm airs and all the Juney things. The air is a-quiver now with the smell of pinks. I take my afternoon nap in the vinery surrounded by a subtle perfume which at first we couldn't place at all. It was the grape blossom. On Sunday on the daisied grass under the apple trees we sprayed the children with the stirrup pump; they squealed and the cuckoo cucked and the babies laughed. They lay and dried themselves and were sprayed again. It all went so much to Roger's head that he took off all his clothes, got through the gap in the hedge and ran naked down the road, and was promptly sent to bed.

In the middle of it all Rita has given notice, or perhaps you could say we have. Her work deteriorated so much that we didn't really know whether she was there to work for the adults or play with the children. One day after Nana and I had been back to tea at Fernlea, we returned to find her sitting among the children in the garden, tea-things scattered in the grass, one baby on her knee and a large chamberpot decorating one of the drive pilasters. There were increasingly other such contretemps, but after our mutual giving of notice her work improved so much that I was tempted to give her another chance. The official at the hostel breezily blew that all away. Rita had always intended to go to her brother's in Kent when she was eighteen and go she would. So everyone is happy and Rita sings her way to bed. As her notice ambles to an end we have

notified various officials and relations including a stepmother who has turned up in her life, and everyone seems to be falling over herself to give Rita a New Start, except Rita herself, who does nothing.

Meanwhile we've advertised for another help. I drafted the advertisement carefully for a couple of papers: 'Wanted: domestic help, for pleasant house with children,' hoping that that described the situation fairly subtly, without giving too much away.

'You don't say,' commented Nicola, 'a house with pleasant children.' No-oo, perhaps not.

By lunchtime the midday edition of the evening paper was out, and there was an avalanche of applicants for the job, so many that at one time I was letting them out of the back door just in time to let the next into the front. After tea a Mrs Rivett came, a person rather out of the usual run. I took her - I think she may prove an institution. Plump, jolly-looking, forthright, and mother of two secondary school girls, she starts on Monday.

Today we found Rita's remains, a bootbox full of underclothing in various stages of decay. Poor Rita; so completely harebrained that she didn't even realise they would be found or so casual she didn't care. We stuffed them on the bonfire, the last and most insalubrious reminders of Rita. Now we await, swept and garnished, the arrival of Mrs Rivett.

† † †

July 7th

As I write we have survived two weeks of Mrs R., two superefficient weeks. We have been spring-cleaned and turned out and scoured and chivvied.

'Am I in your way, Mrs Rivett?'

'Yes.'

'Can I come into the dining-room now, Mrs Rivett?'

'No.'

Well, we know where we are. She's a powerful worker and works me too, and should have been the one to have chivvied Rita. She stood surveying the girl's room, tidied up by me ready for cleaning (I thought) and announced:

'She ought to have been made to clean this out, a young girl like that. I can't do all I want to do to this house in the time I've got, it's just a mad rush round. I'd sooner do one room properly, it'd be fairer to me.'

I agreed wholeheartedly, but as we have ten rooms plus bathroom it was going to be mathematically impossible each week. So now she does one room and I rush round like a maniac doing the others, being fair to Mrs Rivett.

July 18th

I must be just. Mrs R. has turned out to be stimulating as well as forceful. We find we have interests in common like journalism and acting, though my days as amateur actress and producer now seem to belong to that Other Life. Nevertheless we exchange lively reminiscences over the housework, neither of us sitting down long enough to enlarge on anything but throwing anecdotes at each other on the wing. Nana enjoys these exchanges and adds her own cut-and-thrust so there are now three extroverts in the kitchen. Mrs R. is gently edging me towards doing some lecturing, if I may use so euphemistic a term.

'Can't you give a talk to my drama group on the work of a producer?' she tackled me one day. Obviously when she says, 'Can't you?' she means you can, so I thought it over and supposed I could before my drama experience got cold, and within a week I had drafted it out. It seems there may be other talks in the pipeline like 'The Diary of a Harassed Housewife' as I am becoming an expert on being harassed, and who can tell where it may end.

Mrs R. is good with the children too in a constructive way. When she wants to sweep the kitchen she ups with Jo and Penny and sits them on the table and teaches them nursery rhymes while she moves the chairs round and they don't dare to move, either of them. She polishes the floor so well with my home-made polish (an economy measure) that I am having to make little Vim pathways to the door to save Nana from slipping over.

† † †

July 22nd

We have celebrated the last child's birthday of the extended family with Janet's birthday yesterday. She was six, and everyone tipped up handsomely for the occasion. I made her a sugar pink gingham dress and the highlight of the day was Geoffrey's model yacht, on which Roger cast an engineer's eye and which we all trooped off to Eaton Park pond to launch. But when the boat was be-calmed in the middle of the enormous pond there were quarrels and tears of disappointment, so once it had finally drifted back to us I deemed it diplomatic to set off for home and birthday tea, the sight of jelly and ice cream soothing most childish ferments.

Janet's birthday rounds off a kind of shaking-down period. It seems that once you've had your first celebration and blown out the candles you are part of the family. I notice too a jelling of the relationships; it is no longer them and us, it is just us. The nieces are more proprietorial than six months ago, accepting that this is now their home and its belongings are their belongings, which seems a healthy state of affairs.

Penny is more self-sufficient. Her attitude towards shut doors has changed: she no longer stands impotent, crumpling up her face and howling. She has probably learnt to turn the handle but whatever it is, it is an improvement. Joanna's reaction is characteristic: she rattles the handle until it sounds like falling off, and kicks the paintwork for good measure, so we all rush and open it to save the fabric generally.

Roger, now leader and orderer-about, has gone up in the pecking order and bosses the girls about 'something awful' according to Nicola. Today being rainy I can hear him organising some kind of spectacular in the

49

living-room. When I shout to ask what's going on, Nicola pokes her head round the door ...

'We're playing nursing homes and Roger's the doctor. Don't suspect anything if you hear Sue crying, she's just going to be born.'

Roger's authoritative tones then boom out:

'Good morning, Mrs Smith, what can I do for you?'

'I want my baby born.'

'Certainly madam, that'll be thruppence. I'll just get my hearing aid...'

'Steffoscope, silly.'

'And my white overall...'

'Well hurry up. I've got to do my shopping.'

'You're always in a hurry. Jus' wait and I'll born her,' and there comes a noise like the popping of a champagne cork.

'There you are, she's borned!'

And the next minute in a piping treble, Sue, having obviously entered this world, cries. M'm. Seems as if my attempts at sex education have borne fruit in more ways than one. Imagination, nevertheless, boggles at what happened in between. No doubt Roger is behind it all. He has a keen awareness of all things feminine and is at present very attached to his matronly teacher, Miss Whybrow. He eyed me critically one day when I was wearing a Sloppy Joe jumper which I admit hung on me as a scarecrow.

'Miss Eyebrow had one on like that,' said he, 'but hers hadn't got any wrinkles in it, 'cos she's got two big spots in front to fill it up.'

Lucky Miss Eyebrow.

'Why haven't you?'

'Because I rush round looking after ten people, that's why.'

'You shouldn't ever rush round. Let someone else do the work then you'll have big spots too.'

I might, but it's highly doubtful. I'm just not a big spotter.

At six, Roger's front teeth are beginning to come out, the last one being precipitated by bumping into a Big Girl. As each child gets sixpence for losing a tooth he was quick on the mark asking for it.

'So can I have my sixpence?'

'If you produce the tooth, yes. No tooth, no sixpence.'

'I can't. I looked for it, but it was difficult to see in the playground among the other white things.'

'What white things? It's an asphalt playground.'

'Bits of paper and... and... stones and things. Anyway, it was there yesterday and it's not there today. Look!'

Well, where else can a tooth go but out? I gave him his money.

† † †

August 18th 1950

But life isn't quite all work. We have, at last, arranged a visit back to Platters so that the nieces, Janet at least, can keep contact with Geoff and the boat. Penny is still a bit small to travel. It raised some problems, but in the end we arranged the trip in instalments, Janet and Roger going north with Nana for a week and I replacing Nana later.

I was glad to go, having just worked through the twenty-fourth clinic since Easter, and at Norwich Thorpe Station I felt an unearthly sense of freedom. Four hours' sitting down without nappies or noses! A week away from hospitals, washing and mayhem in the kitchen, the battle for supremacy of the sink going on without me. Nirvana!

As the train left the Wash and ran up through Yorkshire and Durham, the flat green lands giving place to the grey sprawl of industry, I felt an acute sense of excitement and nostalgia. On Tyneside, where I took my first post, beauty and industrialisation had always existed side by side. Only half a day's walk from the shipyards and engineering works were quiet villages where the South Tyne trickled beside bluebell drifts and trout streams, past woods smelling of wild garlic and beyond to the eternal moors. Could five years of war, which had brought prosperity to those desolate inner areas, have brought some urban improvement with it, I wondered? If so, it would be a miracle after the blitz they suffered.

But the war had not left Newcastle any more beautiful than I remembered it. How could it? In this, a city I had loved and where I had spent five years, I felt today a distaste for the shoddiness of everything. In this blustery rainy August there were few signs of summer, no colour in the clothes, no tanned skins, no summer carefreeness; only turbaned heads, dun-coloured coats, grey legs, making their wearers indistinguishable from the pavements they walked on. And yet it had always been so; I had simply forgotten. Here, poverty and a cruel climate had always to be fought against. It was for their laughter and their guts I had loved the Geordies, not for their urban surroundings.

In Newcastle I caught a local train out to the coast. At Seaton Sluice, where the boat was moored under the lee of the hill just as Anne had

51

described it, the two children tumbled out to meet me. Janet, bubbling with excitement, showed me her little bedroom, the ramp where she used to play with Penny, and the beach over the grassy hill; we gazed with affection at the little school where she went in her brown buttoned boots with Billy Brady and the girl from the coastguard's cottage on the cliff. No mention of mother.

The next day, going back into Newcastle in the needling rain with Geoff and the children, I made tracks for my old digs in Byker. Here in the dark streets by the river I had looked for greenery in the spring and found none, except an almond tree that flowered in a churchyard along City Road beside the Tyne and the clanking trams. For to experience the changing seasons you had to take a different tram to that beautiful ravine, Jesmond Dene, its wildness tamed into a public park. But that was half an hour distant and we were off today to visit my ex-landlady, Belle Tweddle, living no more in the old friendly hugger-mugger Byker that spilled down to the river, but on the new estate into which she moved in my last year. We waited on her dripping doorstep, wondering whether to knock again or to decamp and get out of the wind, but suddenly the door opened and Belle welcomed us full of delight.

She gathered us up, apologising for the clutter, 'For I'm late back from Assumption Day Mass, me darlins, but come in, come in, ye're welcome as the flowers in spring.' Warmth radiated from Belle and the roaring fire alike. We hugged each other and I presented Roger and Janet and she marvelled and we reminisced and drank coffee and the children crunched sticky sweets and thirteen years dissolved away without trace.

We had to tear ourselves away eventually to lunch with Geoff in the gaunt shadow of the High Level Bridge; after that it was too wet to dally so we fought the black rain all the way back to the coast.

But the weather next day was transformed and we awoke to clear rainwashed skies. Geoff hired the village taxi and we set off after breakfast to explore the coastal villages on the way to the border: Craster, Seahouses, Bamburgh. In Craster a young girl was hanging out sheets beside her front path, brilliant white sheets tortured by the wind and exposed for all to see. An especially fiendish gust would have blown them out to sea. No sheltered walled gardens here it seemed, just trippers and boats, crabs for sale, wind and screaming gulls. What did Belle find to do here summer after summer, for all about was dark stone, steel sea, twisted trees and searing gales, in spite of the sun. And yet there was a kind of strength about it all which had spawned a fearless people, and a savage beauty which, apart from the shrieking elements, reminded me of balmier Cornwall.

About midday we left the wild sunny coast and struck inland to parkland, bridging the green denes and on to the moors, in front of us the Cheviots, now chequered in sun, now lost in cloud. We dipped into Chillingham to see the famous herd of white cattle but found instead an oasis of quiet among green trees and the clear tinkle of a burn fording the road. We dallied here, glad to be out of the wind, and the children, released, paddled in the burn, though it meant more to Roger as a motor splash than a pastoral ford. And so on to Rothbury my beloved in its amphitheatre of hills, where we drank steaming tea and munched on scones and jam.

In the late afternoon we turned for home by way of Warkworth, where years before I had pushed in the shallow stony river the boats of the school children from the school camp, who had never seen a small boat, didn't know how to row and were going round in circles. We also stopped at a café (yes again), where a woman with a soft Northumbrian burr gave us handfuls of Beauty of Bath apples, and showed us where they grew, in a walled garden so brilliant with nasturtiums and dahlias that it seemed exploding with sunshine.

And so back to Platters as the shadows grew long.

† † †

We finished the week in and around the houseboat, searching for shells and tiny marine creatures in the rock pools, tea-ing at the coastguard cottage and with those who had, even so briefly, known Anne, so that Eaton End and its problems seemed very far away. But in spirit of course it was always waiting, and the day came when Janet had to say goodbye to Platters a second time. It was I who left subdued.

Geoff had assembled a scrap-book of the story of the boat from the first advertisement of it in the Woodbridge paper to the notice of Anne's death. In it were Anne's own article, some photos, many newspaper cuttings, in all a record of high hopes. It was perhaps inevitable that he should include Matthew Arnold's much-loved 'Requiescat':
> 'Strew on her roses, roses,
> And never a spray of yew...'

53

but among the pages towards the end was a quotation I didn't know, from Marie Hartley's 'Yorkshire Heritage':

'It is as though we had been tossed into a great wave that had swept her out to sea, but left me floundering in the backwash of a receding tide - the shore strange, the prospect lonely.'

† † †

October

The year weakens. A gale is blowing, the walnut trees are bare and it rains a warm enervating rain. Mrs Rivett has asked me to produce the play I have written for her Guild as she is probably giving up drama. A depressing thought: I had hoped to sit back myself and have it produced, having no desire to leap into the maelstrom of production again.

November

A newspaper bill dropped into the letterbox this morning: 'Peterborough Advertiser. Nov. 7th. In Memoriam insert. Grant. 7/3d.'

All that remains of Anne, except for the children of course. It is two years since we came to Norwich in the thick grey fog and today it is again dripping and the sky leaden. I too am leaden, a return to the old exhaustion, stretched screaming muscles, backache and a prickle in the limbs. How long, O Lord, is the hospital list now?

Janet has chicken-pox and the entire six youngsters are tucked away in various parts of the house. Well, we are lucky to be able to tuck them away. Roger looks as if he may be sickening for it too, but contrary to what all the medical leaflets say, he has developed a prodigious appetite. I went down early one morning to make the porridge and found the pantry light on. Two dirty-soled feet and a pyjama-ed behind twitched under the kitchen table. Roger, of course, marauding.

December

Christmas, oh Christmas! We are gradually preparing for it again, the first one all together and therefore rather special. I have the great idea of pooling all the relatives' contributions and buying a large play-slide which might mop up some of the surplus energy zinging around just now, chicken-pox or no chicken-pox.

Christmas 1950

I did just that. And on Christmas Eve, after hiding packages away for weeks, we stacked all the presents in four large pillowcases and Nana's big linen-bag with the peacock feather pattern on it and stealthily erected the play chute. At eleven o'clock we called the snoozing elder children and all went down to Midnight Mass, me with a hot water bottle under my coat to combat the icy chill of the huge church.

What would we do without the holly and the ivy, the crib and the tall candles, the splash of scarlet cassocks against cream stone, and the high sweet melody of the carols swelling to the vaulting above; in fact, without the whole uplifting ceremony of the First Mass of Christmas? To me, it never fails; it is a healing after all the worldly preparations of our twentieth-century Christmas. Even the young ones share in the wonder of it, despite cold toes, and make the most of that lovely moment when they can go to the crib and relive once more the story of Bethlehem. Emotional, yes, but what is the spiritual if divorced from the emotions? Didn't Pascal say the heart had its reasons?

We came back at half-past one to the traditional mincepies and hot drinks and then bundled everybody off to bed for a brief night's sleep.

At dawn on Christmas morning there were sounds of merriment upstairs and going up to peep through the door I was faced with a scene of near-chaos topped with a cloud of wrapping-paper and I crept back to bed again before anybody saw me. It wasn't long then before Joanna woke and we brought her into our bed to open her presents, her first real Christmas. Ecstatic moment to watch the wonder unfold; the fumbly undoing of the bright paper, the concentration, the gradual dawning of joy in those clear blue eyes. We would not see it again. She was absorbed in the hammer toy we had bought, which we thought a change from hammering the furniture, and the cardboard untearable book, and the chocolate. But what really took her attention were Penny's presents, the six round little wooden men in a cart, her barrel-shaped posting-box and the rocker. Obviously we've underestimated Joanna's abilities; perhaps she should have more sophisticated, rumbustious toys.

Once downstairs, Janet was thrilled with her secondhand trike, now painted green, but for Roger and Nicola the highlight was the chute. They climbed it, slid down it forwards, backwards, curled up, two together, pushed the young ones down when they dithered at the top and finally, screaming with joy, decanted all the toys down it. What a superb recipe for wet days! I could feel the recent tension drain away as I watched them.

Sue, by contrast, was in a happy dream with her 'smelling bottle' that somebody had the inspiration to give her. She went round quietly dowsing everything with scent, looking quite unlike a perfumed femme fatale in her solid square-toed shoes and woollen socks, beguiling us with her chatter and sparkling eyes, and clutching to her chest the adored doll that Father Christmas had brought her.

And then surprise, surprise! Suspicious noises having been heard from the top attic, Roger went to investigate. A large cloud of eiderdown unfolded and there was Geoff, blinking at the daylight, having arrived at three in the morning again on a coaling boat from the North.

And so to the first year's end. Very different from its beginning, measly and moving. On the day after Boxing Day we had a children's party. Twelve assorted young neighbours screamed through the house and threw buns at the wall and each other. I made a cake in the shape of an engine which I thought ingenious and Roger thought scientifically incorrect but which soon got eaten up.(If unscientific, destroy the evidence.) And Auntie Bea made a huge cardboard dog and filled it with gifts, a clever piece of post-war do-it-yourself that probably only I appreciated.

On New Year's Eve when the general celebrations were waning, James and I flopped in armchairs by the sinking fire.

'The occasion demands a toast,' said James, opening the last bottle of Christmas wine. 'Do you realise we have survived a year?'

'I do indeed. And yet... it's not really the year past we should be drinking to. We've weathered that. It's the future.'

'If we thought too much of the future, we'd drink ourselves under the table,' rumbled James. 'Fill up.'

'That's an idea,' said I, slightly bibulous by this time. 'Let's.'

So, among the holly and the ivy, we did.

‡   ‡   ‡

December 1951

A year on. Sue has gone to school; Nana has become Nanalou because Joanna cannot pronounce Loomes; Mrs Rivett has become an institution and the cat has had kittens.

I would like to record that we had entered on a period of bursting health among the children and perfect amity in the kitchen but of course we have done no such thing. The hospital visits go on as before and the kitchen still isn't big enough for three of us, psychologically, though I am happy to record that James has ideas of making it larger geographically. I would imagine I am now somewhere about halfway up the hospital list; three years.

What has really made me put pen to paper this bleak December day is that we are battling through another all-time low. The family has been struck by the prevailing dysentery. I suppose epidemics are part of the stuff of life but they are unedifying, unconstructive, uncomfortable in the extreme; particularly in our family where every childish ailment goes through six of us at least and in this last case, eight. It seems that as soon as we lose diphtheria, smallpox, scarlet fever and tuberculosis, we acquire poliomyelitis and dysentery, and I hear that glandular fever and jaundice are gaining ground. Janet was our first patient in November two weeks ago, with what we thought was a normal diarrhoea and sickness but eventually the poor child vomited only mucus and blood. Two days later Penny caught it too. We isolated them from the rest of the household, not really knowing the cause, but by the end of the week Nicola too was in bed; then Sue was sent home very sick and with a temperature, and finally Roger, 'hot in the head'. The next day the doctor diagnosed the lot as Sonne dysentery. It is reaching epidemic proportions in the schools and is spreading among the adult population. The M.O.H. has devised an emergency routine to deal with it. Every suspect is provided with a small bottle and a spatula, and no matter how healthy he may appear to be, has to send in a specimen of faeces at intervals. (James tells us that because the Health Department jib at using the good old Anglo-Saxon word for what they need, they are constantly getting the wrong specimens.) Joanna was our sixth victim, and then one day James came home furious and muttering and feeling unwell, to say that he had succumbed too.

Day-to-day routine at Eaton End is clinical. The patients all have to take largish tablets each day, the kiddies' all-over quota being fifty-seven and James's forty for himself alone. I use a pestle and mortar to crunch the children's tablets and hide them in meat extract or jam sandwiches or any other food they are able to eat, and think, every time I crush one, that there must be a simpler way, and that something attractive like fruity drinks shouldn't be beyond the wit of man to devise. The seven patients are distributed round the house and crawl down to meals as they feel able. To those who can't, meals are taken up. Each day we take a count of those able to eat, and cook accordingly. The remainder of the work Nana and I split up between us. I take the patients, clothes-washing, floor-swabbing and tablet-crushing; Nana a modicum of cooking and the local shopping. Mrs Rivett does everything else. I feel inadequate to relate the frustrations, arguments or weariness entailed. Let us say that everyone does her best according to her lights and some of our lights are dim. Moreover, James, who normally would have been a tower of strength even though most of the time at the office, is out of action.

After two weeks our eighth victim caught it, Mrs Rivett, and I had to send her home objecting strongly because she didn't feel ill at all. To me she was the greatest loss of all. There are no short cuts to nursing an illness like dysentery; the children have to be cleaned up, bedclothes washed and new ones put on, hands held and fears soothed; drinks given in the night and bad dreams interpreted; food made tempting and trays taken up; the fretfulness that follows has to be borne, diverted or channelled into some other interest, and on top of it all there are nine people at home, mostly under par, fractious and quarrelsome, and none of them allowed to mix with their fellow men until every germ is clear.

In the afternoons, when the main chores were done, I crept to my eyrie under the roof, my snug little attic, my hideaway, to sleep. But even here emergencies followed me; either the convalescents ran out into the garden without shoes, or the doctor called, or the Sanitary Inspector. Or no-one answered the door at all and I had to rouse myself and go down two storeys and do it myself. We have all been touchy, James with dysentery, me with exhaustion and Nanalou, who has prodigious energy, with plain natural argumentativeness.

Later

However, little things have illuminated the gloom, Roger's first letter for instance to Nana Barnard:

58

Dear Nana Barnard,
    I here you are at Auntie Joans. I
    DO hope you like the pig's an
    calve's. last Wensday the kitten
    had his eyars open.
    We all have dissantry,
    but doant worry.
              Love, Roger

Both naïve and revealing in one who learned to write so late.

After a fortnight the first patients are beginning to be convalescent and go for little walks. Roger comes bursting in the door with Janet and Sue and yells, 'Mummy! We've got a present for you. Three bunches of wild parsley. Can you put it on the dinner?'

'I should think so.'

'It's a good thing we got a lot, isn't it?' asks Sue. 'There was thousands of it. No-one was picking it.'

'Fine. Let's put it in a jar.' I reflected that last week there was next to no-one eating any dinner to put it on.

They all trot into the kitchen very pleased with themselves. It's all the same to me what decorates the dinner, barring poison. We've had wild parsnip, greater celandine, carrot leaves (feathery) and young nettles and I haven't been above a lupin leaf on occasion.

Apart from letter-writing, Roger has started cooking. Yesterday he shut himself in the kitchen quietly making cakes. He brought the mixture in to us in a big bowl, holding it carefully, and announced it was made 'of corn flakes, some white powder from the pantry, sour milk and water and cocoa'.

'What was the white powder?' we all wanted to know.

'Oh, I don't know, it was in a packet on the shelf.'

I roused myself and went to investigate, guessing that it might be ground rice.

'Was it this one, Roger?'

'Yes,' but he looked shifty. However, someone had to be brave so we dared to taste. H'm. Negative. Could be anything.

'Have you cooked it at all, Roger?'

'Yes, a little.' But I don't think he had. James ate his half manfully. then suggested that it went back into the oven.

'With some sugar,' I suggested.

'Righto,' said Roger, striding off purposefully.

So tomorrow we shall have to eat it.

We have now discovered what the white powder was: wall-filler! An excellent remedy for dysentery. I wonder no-one has thought of it before.

December 20th

We are through, we are almost through. Only Joanna is not clear. We have emerged to find it nearly Christmas again. Nana and I, looking back on the recent carnage, realise that she and I were the only ones who didn't catch it, a miracle if ever there was one.Mrs Rivett turned up one morning full of energy and withering invective against the M.O.H. 'I suppose he knows what he's doing, lot of red tape. Anyway, I'm here. Now what have you got for me to get on with? Everything, from the look of things. Don't know how you'd ever get on without me.'

'It's all yours,' I said.

February 1952
Pond Farm

Joanna's dysentery like the melody lingered on... and on. But by the end of January she also was clear. Eight weeks of coping with it had left me a near-skeleton and it was decided that I go to Joan's farm for a rest. She could, I hoped, tuck us away in a corner somewhere without unduly noticing us. 'We' included Joanna, who would be nicely intrigued with the animals and wouldn't be at Eaton End to incite the others to riot.

So here I am at Joan's. It is midwinter and the fields around are in the grip of frost. Every day, for a short while, this melts into mud, right up to the door of the kitchen, where the farm hands and Matthew, Joan's husband, leave their enormous knee-boots leaning against each other like drunken men. No-one dare cross Joan's kitchen floor in boots. The kitchen itself is enormous and sparkling clean and warm and full of good smells. The most delectable meals come forth from the Aga. Today we had woodcock (or golden plover, they couldn't agree, but it tasted superb), and in the evening, pigeon and rabbit. It's a refreshing change

60

from Spam and corned beef, and the inevitable apple tart. Counteracting
the awful weather came another ray of sunshine from Roger...

> to Joanna and mummy   Norwich
> Dear mummy,
> > I hope you are having a
> > nice rest and that Joanna
> > is not to naughty.
> > Nicola is being mummy
> > insted of you, and Dad
> > is very strict.
> > onlee I Downt thingk you will
> > like this that the king died
> > in his sleep last
> > wenesday.
> > > Love from
> > > Roger

February 26th

Back home I was in time for Roger's birthday, for which he had a cake
shaped like a figure eight, and raked in five shillings from Aunt Georgina
by post and the same from Nana B. He was very pleased about this
windfall and asked me for half-a-crown of it to go and buy something for
Nanalou whose birthday follows his. Poor Nana, she can rarely manage
to celebrate it out of Lent. This year it will fall on Ash Thursday, as you
might say.

As I fetched Sue home from school, I saw Roger wandering
nonchalantly to town. 'Shan't be long,' said he off-handedly, 'jus' going
down to the market.' When he returned for tea we were all in the middle
of eating Shrove Tuesday pancakes, so I asked him surreptitiously what
he had bought for Nana. 'Oh some grapes and brussels sprouts. Come up
and see them, they're in my room.'

We went up conspiratorially. On the top of his wardrobe was a large
jam-jar full of snowdrops ('sixpence a bunch, three bunches'), a pound of
onions, a bag of cress and a tin of white grapes which itself must have
cost two shillings.

'I got them all on the market,' he said proudly. 'Do you think they are
all right?'

I was somewhat at a loss for words. However...

'They're lovely. But I don't think the cress will last till Thursday, it's rather delicate stuff. What about giving it to Nana today?'

'Good idea. It's a bit hot too, isn't it? I had a taste,' and he clattered downstairs to give it to Nana, who was quite overwhelmed. But wait till she sees the onions.

March 7th

On the home front we soldier on.

Penny, of the reproachful brown bumblebee eyes, who couldn't say shoo to a hen, and Joanna, have a field day every afternoon when I am napping and Nana isn't noticing. The list of their misdemeanours includes such choice items as:-

Throwing some two dozen lumps of coal on to the lawn.

'Penny and me wanted to make a bonfire like Dad.'

Marching down the road dishevelled and snotty, Joanna pushing the decrepit pram.

'Just takin' my baby for a walk,' says Joanna when challenged. 'Penny's my nursemaid.'

Filling with stones Nana's clean white counterpane, looped up on the line.

Pouring water on the kitten and digging up the soil carefully put there in a trough for plants.

Getting into bed at midday and putting on each other's nighties.

Sitting on Roger's bed, unravelling his precious bus ticket rolls, while Penny, with a conductor's set round her neck, clips the ravellings. A child guidance clinic couldn't provide better uninhibited activity.

Bottoms up

On Tuesday I took a pale and gumboily Nicola to the dental clinic, where she has had two teeth extracted with gas. She swore she hadn't been asleep, couldn't eat, and ached all over so I took her to a little cafe nearby resorted to by harassed mothers after dental clinics. She promptly ate a chocolate cake, drank a fizzy lemonade, went on to school and has been as FIT as a FLEA for a whole school week.

Whit Monday

Lovely May into flaming June, six weeks of sunshine. The flowers are still bursting into bloom in chaotic order. The giant poppies are now out and the syringa. And tonight the first heavy summer rain is falling.

Yesterday morning, on being called for Whit Sunday Mass, Sue put her hand down the bed and hauled up a wet ginger kitten, born during the night. I think we should call him Pentecost.

The Sunday before Whit, Janet made her First Communion. On the spiritual side I cannot answer for her but on the physical side we all squashed ourselves into a taxi to support her. I had made a white dress for her in a soft patterned rayon, and she looked quite charming, especially in the photograph taken afterwards. Previously I had taken her to town to choose a Communion present from her Daddy. She wasn't at all inclined to have a prayer book, in fact turned her nose up at them, so we went up to the picture floor. I reckoned we could find something there that came within the religious category even if on the fringe, but I had a hard twenty minutes persuading her to choose a holy one. In fact I never did. She wanted nursery rhymes first and foremost and nothing would budge her. In the end we got quite a pleasant one of a boy saying grace and she chose it because it looked as near as dammit to Little Tommy Tucker. Then she wanted string on it, so the assistant obliged.

However once having chosen the picture she had no afterthoughts about it and took it to bed with her that night, unhooking it off the wall where we had hung it.

‡ ‡ ‡

Following the Whitsuntide initiation, Janet and Sue have strewn flowers in the Corpus Christi procession, the Thursday after Trinity. Strewing is a ritual, first involving the decoration of tall-handled baskets. We wind white ribbon round the handle (everything is white for Corpus Christi) and finish with a bow, or even two, where the handle joins the bowl, tucking the flowers between the weaving to make an edging. This is a concentrated job to be done on the day itself lest the flowerheads wilt. There is in June a predominance of white pinks or marguerites or tiny climbing roses. If we use the roses we tear the delicate blooms apart along with lilac heads, and in a late spring the mock-orange adds its perfume, heady and overwhelming, to the general bouquet.

The strewer usually watches the basket-decorating process with restrained excitement, tempered by a critical eye, for her basket must be appropriate to the occasion and at least as good as those of her fellow-strewers (the human element to the fore, you'll notice). Then we put it in the coolest place, like the flagged courtyard, to be protected till procession time.

Meanwhile we have been getting together the white dress and veil. Sue's was of parachute nylon, one of Nicola's, delicately creamy, and the veil was of tulle crowned with tiny roses, and you can take it from me that wearing a white tulle veil is one of the most exciting experiences in life: it simply makes the wearer beautiful. There then only remained the white shoes and socks and the job of getting down to the Church Hall early so that they might be in the right order for strewing under the benevolent eye of Miss Russell.

Having done all this, we the parents file into the back of the church and we wait, with the keenest anticipation, for the procession to begin.

Here they come. There is a stir at the west door and the first acolyte with the cross emerges from the press of people. I get a temporary shock at the sight of James among the processors, resplendent in purple and black, looking halfway between a barrister and a Roman senator, either of which roles would have suited him admirably. Later enquiries reveal that he and others similarly garbed are members of the Blessed Sacrament Guild and when I chided him afterwards for not preparing me for such splendour he assured me he didn't know either. Indeed this regalia is as striking as the gowns of the City Officials and if anyone were to take issue with the Church for its worldly garb I could only say that men will dress up whether in or out of religion.

And then come the strewers, preceding the canopied Host, intent on kissing and dropping their petals and only occasionally having a stare round to see if mother is there. Janet sees me every time she comes round but Sue is more intent on her strewing. I am forced to admit that Janet is a material little person, and things she cannot see, or even less imagine, do not mean very much to her. Her Christianity is dead practical, but who can really complain of that? I am quite unrepentant in thinking that, in England anyway, we could make more of these milestones in their lives.

Lastly, home, cornflakes and to bed, everyone tired.

When they are all up in the bathroom on the last exhausting lap, a phone call comes through to 'Mrs Grant'. I answer automatically. A woman's voice introduces herself as a Scout mistress down at the church and says, 'I've found a child here who says she is Penny Grant. She says her family have gone off and left her behind, so I'm just ringing up...'

'O.K., O.K., we'll be down immediately, many thanks...'

We take a count: Roger, Nicola, Sue, Janet, Joanna... yes, number six *is* missing. It is the only occasion, so far, we've mislaid a child.

╪   ╪   ╪

June

There is much traffic in jars and bright flowers among the children because of the very early summer; eschscholtzia flares all over the house and the smell of pinks is overpowering. Among it all the lone kitten, Pentecost, squeaks and squeaks. Its mother, our usual faithful tabby, has left it and it can't lap. Although there are several human fostermothers trying to feed it with spoons the squeak goes on.

Today I had my long-awaited appointment with the gynaecologist, a pleasantly professional man who tried to put me at ease. Apparently the ravages on one's innards of producing children can be tidily pleated up with no trouble at all, but no-one knows how much longer I shall have to wait for the doing of it on the National Health. Mothers seem to be second-class citizens in this year of 1952 and the existence of large families is not really admitted to be quite respectable, let alone worthy of priority. Now in ancient Malta I should have been a fertility goddess.

August 24th 1952

Geoff has been to see us again - he has had an interview for a post in Singapore, a good one, and I think he will take it if it is offered. He came to talk things over and see what we felt about it. I tried to put forward the view that he should keep near his children but obviously he has drifted away from them in the last two years. He is disappointed that I haven't been able to take them north more often. Well, I am disappointed too, but we cannot work the impossible.

65

I asked, 'Suppose we emigrate ourselves?' James had been talking of Canada or Kenya. Geoff suggested that the children be then put into a boarding school here in England, or in Australia, where the British in Singapore usually send their children. Or that they could go with us wherever we went, if we were willing. Fatter, more contented, always hail-fellow-well-met, I get the feeling that Geoff is goodnaturedly shedding his role of father.

February 7th

The new year, always full of hope as far as I am concerned, has early on brought tragedy. Floods have devastated the East Coast, seeping into even our domestic existence, filling the lounge, not with water, but with clothes and bedding. It was on a Saturday night that the storm burst, that of January 31st and February 1st, a wild night and sleeting, with the wind high. We were glad to go to bed and pull the bedclothes up and listen to the gale's menacing roar, shuddering even then at the thought of those out in it. But no-one conceived the devastation that was being wrought hourly all along the East Coast and Holland. The storm coincided with a phenomenal spring tide, doing unimaginable damage. The sea and the rivers, the Wash, Breydon Water and the Thames broke through their banks, sea walls and fortifications, swept over dunes and mudflats and poured into the coastal villages.Mablethorpe and Sutton-on-Sea in Lincolnshire, Cley and Salthouse, Sea Palling and Snettisham in Norfolk were partly swept away, and the death toll was heavy. Towns like King's Lynn, Hunstanton, Yarmouth and Felixstowe and the whole of Canvey Island were deeply flooded, and casualties, especially at Canvey which had nothing to protect it, were heavy. Even Lowestoft, so close, was swamped and without gas or electricity and the sea rushed through Tuttle's drapery shop and Uncle Bert's grocery store, smashing to smithereens the beach huts in its onslaught. It also swept away three hundred beach bungalows at Hunstanton and Heacham, and the tea hut on the dunes at Wells-next-the-Sea was carried three miles.

There were many tragedies. The 'Daily Mirror' gave photos of bodies flung in trees. Sea Palling produced an appalling case of a family in a cottage on the dunes. A row of cottages and all their inhabitants were drowned save one man. He had retreated upstairs with his family until the gable end of the house fell out, when they were all precipitated into the flood. They remained huddled in the icy water until the three children were one by one swept away or died from exposure. The wife was the last to disappear. A week later the baby was washed up.

The main impact of the tides hit Holland where fifteen hundred are already dead and most of the islands inundated. One sixth is already under water. The ravenous sea, reclaiming the land that was reclaimed, has avenged itself.

The tail end of it all has filtered its way down to Eaton End. The local Round Table meeting was cancelled and the men rustled up lorries and vans and went round the houses soliciting clothes, cooking pots, carpets and even brooms, and our house became a collecting centre. Molly McDougal brought her entire layette, having resigned herself to never being able to use it, and old Dow, the builder, brought all his dead wife's clothes. Stewart McDougal went down with a carful of men to Sea Palling to help build up the gap in the sea defences. The response everywhere was terrific. As Lady Reading of the W.V.S. said ironically, 'Even people who could well spare clothes gave this time.'

But there emerged incredible tales of suffering: families were marooned on roofs, men and animals thrown into trees; householders woke up to a mighty thundering to find nothing but sea between them and Europe. The Norfolk coastal area being peppered with American Air Force bases, the U.S.A.F. also played its part, as one would expect. One airman, seven feet tall, pushed a raft through innumerable back gardens to rescue stranded occupants of houses, notwithstanding the fences, hills and hollows in between, and survived to be the saviour of the hour.

'Dead or alive?' demanded his father in America on being told by reporters that his son was a hero.

February 14th

It has taken time for the horrors of the flooding to subside but gradually some sort of order is taking over and there is a desperate attempt to return to normal. All down the east coast carpets are hanging on lines in the weak February sunshine and hundreds of ordinary folk are counting the cost in lives, bricks and mortar, and animals.

But in spite of the tragedy life does return to normal. Today is Valentine's Day and we are gradually back to the small domestic celebrations again.

Nicola has come into the bedroom, clutching a small bag of sweets. 'I couldn't get you a Valentine card and I couldn't get any daffodils 'cos they're too expensive, two and nine a bunch, and a box of chocolates was too dear so I got you these. They're liquorice noogah and they'll be good for your cough!' (I haven't a cough.) 'And the lady says they're very nice. She says it's Mothering Sunday soon and she'll have some snowdrops then.' So we share out a liquorice nougat each and munch away like a couple of conspirators.

Just as well, it will be some time before the next celebration. I had my notification for hospital today, March the first, over four years since it was first mooted. Perhaps we should celebrate that.

February

Meanwhile on the lecturing front, 'The Diary of a Housewife' has become more harassed and Mrs Rivett is gently nudging me to extend the subject range.

'What about Fashion for a change,' said she, 'and to the whole guild, not just the drama group?' What is there I can say about Fashion, I argued, that the sixty ladies present won't know just as well. Much better to ask the member who spent three hours at the Dior salon.

'She can't lecture,' said Mrs R., 'and besides you can bring a roll of drawings like you usually do and liven things up a bit.'

The drawings were large sketches running the length of a roll of wallpaper. I thought it over and as usual compromised. But it was as The Gentle Art of Camouflage that it finally emerged, covering most of the feminine ploys and some of the male ones, from make-up to posture. It was the posture that got them in the end, little weaknesses that needed camouflaging, the angular elbows, stooping shoulders, prominent noses and receding chins, bottoms that stuck out when pram-pushing, feathers that wobbled, tums that protruded. Poise was paramount, I insisted, the outside needing to stand erect while the inside is putting its feet up.

Who am I kidding, I asked myself, but there was no doubt that the audience was happy to be kidded.

Nevertheless, I find myself doing rather too many odd jobs for Mrs Rivett in spite of an inner reluctance. Her usual gambit is, 'You've got more time than me,' and my usual gambit is to stick my heels in. But last week I agreed to chase up a guild member who hadn't turned up for the last rehearsal and was wanted for the next.

Mrs O'Leary came to the door in an apron, looking defeated by life, which was apparently the type of character she had to play. On hearing my message she prevaricated.

'Well I di'n't think I'd go to rehearsal today, I've got such a bad code. Couldn't see out of my eyes Friday. People don't thank you for giving them codes, do they, and I di'n't want anyone to fall out of the play through me. Not that I really need rehearsing, I know my part all right, that's all that matters, isn't it? Did you see the play? Well don't you think it's an awful part, not a bit like me? I'm not miserable like that. Did you hear what the judge said at the competition? That I was a walking

69

corpse? Isn't that awful! A walking corpse! It was in the paper too. Yes, perhaps I will get a different part next time, something lively, more like me. I'm a very lively person really, must be the Irish in me.

'I'm sure it's very good of you to come round. I don't know your name, do I? Oh! you must be the one with all those babies. Fancy, all those babies, six isn't it? How do you manage? Well, yes, I suppose some of them are growing up a bit, but people oughtn't to be expected to bring up all those children, ought they?

'Well, thank you for coming, but I don't think I ought to pass round this code. Perhaps I'll just pop in and see how I feel.'

But she didn't.

March 18th

So we got round to hospital at last. With my bag packed, all lists made, Sue despatched to stay with Aunt Constance and Joanna to Nana's, assurances from my doctor that I would emerge a new woman, and with the feeling that the next three weeks were out of my hands, I arrived at Wayland hospital. I counted fifteen beds in the ward, it being an overflow to the main hospital in Norwich, and I was allocated the corner bed against the kitchen wall, so that when everyone else had cold feet I had warm.

When I came to from the anaesthetic and explored myself I found the surgeon had thrown in (for good measure?) a haemorrhoid operation that was certainly not on my list but was on that of my neighbour, a Mrs Travers. As she had not had it, we both came to the conclusion that the cards had been muddled, until we were informed that my additional operation was merely a precautionary measure and would save me a lot of trouble. What the lack of hers saved Mrs T. I never found out.

A prolapse operation is more miserable than lethal, but a haemorrhoids added to it can be sheer torture, the difficulty being going to the toilet. More sweat, tears and blood were shed in that ward of supposedly simple operations than one could imagine. I found myself ministering comfort to distraught patients all around me and so had little time to brood myself. But after ten days the after-effects had lessened, leaving only a soreness, loss of weight and uselessness in the limbs.

In the second week I could enjoy visitors, which are quite a subject in themselves. My neighbour entertained four at a time, chatting vigorously the while, her face getting hotter and her visitors more vegetable as time

70

went on, because once the hospital bus decants people at Wayland they have to stay for the whole afternoon. Towards the end of the session she began to resemble a red cabbage, pickled at that, or perhaps a balloon that threatened to go off pop. I felt exceedingly sorry for her; she needed the company but she didn't need the amount of time they stayed. The whole point of visitors, I thought, watching the pantomime, is that they should entertain us, not we them. We should be regaled by someone who is the life and soul of the party, but then, I reflected, it would probably cause a rupture of the stitches and so where would you be?

I had a sneaking sympathy with the guests, too, chairless for an hour and a half. But I doubt if you could keep them away from their mothers, brothers-in-law, or grannies, and the patients would fret if they didn't come. Lack of visitors means lack of status. Meanwhile the small children, poor little beggars, had to mouth and wave through the window.

By the second week we were having some fun in the evenings when most of the nurses' work was done. Rosie, a bent grey little person from Railway Street, was the butt of the ward's kindly ragging. Consolations like perms and the National Dentistry service had passed Rosie by. She managed with one tooth and a lot of cheerfulness, and what she lacked in hair style she made up for in pink and blue earrings which she wore continuously except for the operation. She was proud of the earrings: 'From Samuel's,' she said. 'Can't stand any o' them Woollie's things, common, they are. You've gotta buy joolry from somewhere decent.'

Rosie had a stocky husband the same size as herself, and two sons, Young George and Boy Timber. Boy Timber was a cow hand and baby of the family, and on enquiry her baby was found to be thirty. Everyone was anxious to see Boy Timber and when he did turn up he was the spitting image of his parents. When he left her, Rosie exhorted him not to cry. 'I'll be alright,' she cheered him, weeping copiously as she waved goodbye.

Rosie, battered as she was by life, had an innate modesty. There were things she couldn't show a doctor and she was appalled by the idea of hospital and 'thought the patients wouldn't spik to her'. But as it happened she was the darling of the ward. Gradually we heard her history. She had been everybody's drudge: she had pushed an ailing mother about for years in a wheelchair, and then her husband, Old George, had had rheumatic fever and she had nursed him for eleven years with the aftermath of that. Her main pet was 'my poor punny' who grazed in a field at the back of the old City Station. We gathered it pulled a cart from time to time, probably a rag-and-boner, but we never really knew. We did know that she was pernickety about food. For all her poverty Rosie wouldn't eat such things as restaurant stews (you don't know what's in 'em) or tinned fish or meat, or fish and chips from a shop. 'If you cook 'em yourself you do know what they're made of,' said she.

† † †

April 8th

I was pleasantly cocooned at Wayland for three weeks and two days. Towards the end, James, bringing news of the family whom he assured me were well and in good hands, told me I was to go to Nana Barnard's to begin my convalescence. I looked forward to that with a great lightening of spirit, especially as it included Joanna, a tenuous if turbulent link with home. He also brought me the sad news, half-expected, that the Treasurer, a gentle cultured man, had died, and that he, James, had been offered the post. We sat there thinking that one person's gain is another person's loss and that now a wholly different life was perhaps open to us. We agreed too that any celebrations must be postponed till my return when I might be relaxed enough to appreciate them.

So one rainwashed day I limped into the hospital taxi with several other convalescents and finally, after a winding journey through Norfolk lanes, arrived in Lowestoft for the last stage of being a new woman.

Oulton Broad
April 18th

Time slips away. Here at Meadowfield is the quintessence of spring. The new light floods Nana Barnard's clean little room with the bright fire burning and the dog curled up beside it. Tea is laid on a chequered cloth and a huge jar of forsythia shines in the middle of it like fractured pieces of sunshine. Today I am alone and have time to write and the ideas flow again, which is just as well because last night I felt there was absolutely no progress at all in a week. But commonsense taking over tells me that after such a long slide down there cannot be a quick up, and I shall get an objective report from Nana's doctor and friend, Deene.

72

April 21st

Yes, quite objective. Walking very slowly down the green road at Oulton Broad, I went along to Deene. He was fatherly, held my hand and told me not to whip myself into recovering, gave me some bromide and told me to rest.

'Your mother-in-law,' he beamed, pressing my hand, 'will be in her element getting you better.'

‡ ‡ ‡

Easter has intervened; James sent me a cheque for an Easter bonnet and scribbled on the note with it, 'The house is dead without you.' I spend the days vegetating with Joanna, going for walks, just a little further each day, listening to the W.I. gossip from Cousin Flo', being cosseted by Nana and reading. But it couldn't last. I had been away nearly five weeks altogether and the onus at home was on everybody else. It was time to return to Eaton End.

The children clustered round me asking myriad questions: 'What's it like in hospital? Do they hurt you? Did they put a thing over your face to make you go to sleep? Mary O'Malley's mother went to hospital to have a baby. Do they sew you up again with a needle and cotton? Daddy's made us all tidy up, every day. Why wouldn't they let us come and see you?'

And Roger, cutting through the prattle: 'You've missed Mothering Sunday, so you might as well have the presents now.'

Ah! that was a pleasant surprise. To me Mother's Day is always redolent of violets (begged, borrowed or stolen), of primroses arranged in egg-cups, or wankly little primulas in pots. This year was no exception. With me being away the three little ones had been able to plot and buy in comfort and I thought I detected Nic's judgement behind some of the choices. 'We thought we wouldn't get you the usual things,' said Nicola, 'so we've got you something useful.'

'Useful to you or me?' I asked guardedly.

'Well, for all of us,' giggled Nic, laying on the coverlet a series of bulging parcels.

I opened them cautiously, overwhelmed as always with my own inadequacy. There they lay, six oranges 'for your diet', two half-pounds of biscuits, and a chocolate gateau squiggled with icing. Then Sue came in with daffodils, worried because they were wilting ('I got them on the market'), and we had a conference on flower-revival, and after all that confabulation we all had to have a biscuit so they were a specially useful present after all.

James weighed in with some perfume, 'Indiscret'. Dare one be indiscreet? Is it part of the new woman image?

Nana, not to be outdone, gave us all a cake as a topsy-turvy present, presumably for daughter's day. I thought with a little stab that I hadn't anything for her.

And Sue has learnt a new song; I hear it all over the house in her childish treble:

> A wee little worm in a hickory nut
> Sang happy as he could be:
> Oh I live in the heart of a whole round world
> and it all belongs to me.

May

And that seems like the end of my real convalescence. The nurses were quite right about hurrying slowly; one just can't hurry these things. I had a week of try-as-you-can with Penny being fetched every day from school by someone else, but my first return to housekeeping was pretty disastrous. I have a tremendous urge for one of those motherly souls in novels who say, 'There, there, Miss Mary, just you concentrate on getting better, I'll take *Joanna* care of the chores. Bacon or sausage with your egg?' There ought to be a pool of caring souls for just such emergencies. I reckon we shall have to go back to a full-time liver-in to tide us over the frantic periods, like the bed-and-bathtime flurry.

It has occurred to me that there might be an answer to my dilemma right under my nose. Along the road the hostel for mental health trains girls for domestic work and after a probationary period they are allowed to live in. I think that a visit to Matron might be in order.

It was with considerable reluctance that I made up my mind. I would be sorry to lose Mrs Rivett, who was super-efficient, intelligent, identified with us ('The family can't do without me,' she boasted), and her outside interests in many ways tallied with mine.

James would have made her full-time housekeeper, but James didn't live in the kitchen. There would always be three strong-minded individuals in it. Two too many.

Nana B. summed it up as usual. 'You've got to be mistress in your own house,' said she, 'no matter what.'

It took some days. Once when I had got myself to the sticking-point she had left early and on another occasion a visitor arrived. There has to be a special moment for whipping up the adrenalin. But one morning, feeling pretty low, I downed a glass of sherry, took myself and bottle down to the kitchen and poured out a stiff one for her.

'Have some Dutch courage; you're going to need it. It's no good beating about the bush. I've got to have some full-time help. I am getting a girl to live in.'

Geoff turned up for his final few days before going abroad. He put-puttered into the drive in a rickety old car and took us out for jaunts in the fresh green countryside, some of the best outings we have had in Norfolk. Then he left at the weekend and flew to Singapore. Here I think has ended the second chapter of Geoffrey and Anne.

‡ ‡ ‡

June 1953

Among the phenomenal events overtaking us this year is the end of much of the food rationing, a very liberating experience, making one feel like celebrating with pipe and drum, or a thumping good meal at a restaurant if there weren't so many of us. Up until May this year, our masters the Ministry of Food have de-rationed tea, eggs, chocolates and sweets, home-produced cheese, cooked gammon and ham and any uncooked gammon that's going around, and, miracle of miracles, canned corned beef, a real bonus. For years the allocation of it has been two ounces per person, per week, sometimes four and often none at all, so that as soon as you got used to it as a quick standby, lo! it was snatched away again.

I am more than shocked to count up that rationing has lasted fourteen years already and that still the basics, sugar (12 ounces), butter and

75

margarine (4 ounces each), meat (one-and-tuppence worth), bacon (5 ounces) and imported cheese (none), are in short supply eight years after the war's end. There are rumours that cheese generally, now two ounces per person per week, may be freed next, though the Min. of F. is still dithering over bacon. However in their largesse they gave us each last month an extra four ounces of margarine and a pound of sugar for the Coronation, so that we could all make celebration sponge cakes with real eggs to toast our rather delightful young queen, and precede the sweet with a corned beef and ham salad. A gracious deal!

Ingenuity in making the food rations go round has been one of the major challenges of wartime (and post-war), but I must admit that our family numbers have helped us; there has been more to pool, even though the under-fives were only allowed half the meat ration and no tea. Tea is always stretchable, especially if left on the hob and replenished with boiling water (good for the morale though not the digestion). But for years we went in for breast of lamb with as much stuffing as lamb; or mince, scrag end of mutton, sausage, spaghetti bolognese, or a sausage-meat flan filled with cheesy custard which Roger dubbed 'essage friddle'. Our cauliflower cheeses and spaghetti napolitana had more base than topping. However for ritzy days and celebrations (and we had a few) we went in for brisket, braised for hours on top of the vegetables. Corned beef, when we were allowed it, was an old faithful, but later our real stand-by, worth queueing for, was a tin of Spam, which James with an unerring eye used to slice into nine slivers, so thin you could see the light through them, and heaven help us if we had to cut it into ten for a sudden visitor.

And of course the staple porridge. I hardly dare mention porridge. Like the poor it was always with us; it is even now. James comes down each morning and prepares a huge saucepan of it, doled out with Nana's enormous ladle. The scene is redolent of Oliver Twist, nine or ten of us round the kitchen stove, saucepan plop plopping, plates at the ready, each child eyeing the dollop that splats in front of him/her to see if it's as big as the next one's But unlike Oliver they never ask for more Even camouflaged with brown sugar, syrup, jam or evaporated milk, it is still unchanging porridge.

'When I'm rich,' says Roger, 'I'm going to have cornflakes like the boys at school '

So in the course of time I worked out innumerable substitutes for the foods that disappeared one by one. It wasn't always the foods themselves, but often the ingredients that made them palatable that we missed, like the jam on the bread and the egg in the cake, the mushroom in the casserole, the custard on the apple pie. We shook up the top of the milk in a jar for butter, made carrot marmalade and potato scones and parsnip and marrow ginger jam, worked miracles with dried eggs which wouldn't jell or whip and therefore wouldn't make meringues (if you had sugar) or stick the breadcrumbs to the fish (if you landed some fish). The ways of making ersatz cream were legion.

Alas, cakes and puddings didn't fare so well either. The first of many Christmas puddings in my fading recipe-cuttings book was frugal indeed, must have been around the time of the blitz. Entitled 'Mock Christmas Pudding', its ingredients were stark indeed, and the resultant pudding anything but enticing.

> 1 breakfast cupful self-raising flour
> Half   "   "   suet
> Half   "   "   mixed dried fruit
> 1   "   "   grated carrot
> 1   "   "   shredded potato
> Mix together, add a teaspoonful bicarbonate of soda
> in warm water. Steam or boil. Makes two puddings.

I reckon that must have been a non-starter, eggless, sugarless, flavourless, with the suet and dried fruit as rare as gold, but I must have made it - 'Steam two hours' is written in pencil in the margin.

Little warnings and exhortations used to enliven the end of recipes: 'Stays up two hours;' 'Eat immediately, will not keep', or more optimistically, 'Watch the family wolf this down;' 'Boil this custard for three minutes, your family will love it.' Only those who never knew anything else would love it. But we soldiered on. And when you worked out later that the Dutch (and no doubt the Belgians and French) lived on four-hundred-and-fifty calories a day against our three thousand we didn't fare so badly. But it didn't really seem like it at the time.

Emergence

September 1953

Mrs Rivett has gone and Ellen has come. I could be lyrical about Ellen. She is quiet and wastes no time and she fits in sweetly with the household. She calls me Madam and is, as Matron carefully explained, subservient, and how one's vanity responds to that! She treats the house as my house and me as mistress, which is a change, and there are as yet no emotional barriers between us, no battle of wills. She has been taught to serve and does it well. I feel the resentment and hostility of the last few months washing away.

I opened the door to her one morning after months of trying to cope after the operation, wondering what I should see. On the doorstep stood a pleasant-faced, sturdy girl of twenty-six, smiling tentatively. She said, 'I'm the new help, madam, from the Grange.' Never have I said, 'Come in,' with so light a heart. So Ellen came in and has settled in with the family much as an elder daughter might, fitting in with both young and old in a natural relationship.

The atmosphere in the kitchen these days is strangely serene. I find myself making cakes at ten o'clock in the morning in a room already swept and polished; wet clothes are hung out without fuss in the garden and brought in just right for ironing, and even that, done by her as she talks to the children, is up to Nana's standard. She makes a good nursing orderly too. Nana is at present in bed with gastritis and the doctor has told her to stay there and rest. (Perhaps this is why it is so quiet here below.) Each morning Ellen takes in her tray without asking unnecessary questions and it is accepted without unnecessary instructions. I can hardly believe it is my old chaotic household.

Perhaps I am living in that state of euphoria which always accompanies a new help, optimism always bubbling up, but I have often wondered where Ellen's supposed backwardness lay. Talking to Matron one day I found she had been scooped up into the Grange because she was in need of care and protection. I was mildly surprised at the care, but from the occasional roving look in her eye I could believe in the protection. She lived with her parents in a Norfolk village and was apparently fast descending the downward path; in other words she was after the boys. If that is a form of mental retardedness lots of us must suffer from it.

Ellen likes a bit of horror and on her Wednesdays off she goes to the pictures with the other hostel girls. She comes back and describes the films with gusto.

'I like an X film, Ma'am, I do. I enjoyed that one called THEM. Ooh it was awful, all about great big ants. Every time you chopped their heads off two more grew and they went after the little children. That was the worst bit, because them children got into a dark tunnel like, to get away and couldn't. And ooh, Madam, they did cry. Made me feel quite queer.

'And then, just as these 'ere creatures was going to put their feelers round them they got rescued.

'Then I went to another film last Wednesday, more violent reely that was, not quite like the other. Called JAILBREAK, and Nana she say, doant you go and see that, Ellen. But I went and I enjoyed it, although deep down I was frit, and had to go into Woolworth's arterwards I did, to have a cuppertea and two cream hornets to cheer myself up.'

I think she's happy. We've tucked her away in the little corner attic, sunny and with the luxury of a carpet. But usually being empty there hasn't been much traffic in it lately and it seems the moths have taken over.

So Ellen comes to me round-eyed with a long-drawn-out oo-oh. I know when I hear this owl-call that something is afoot.

'Oo-ooh, madam, all them grubs in the carpet is standing up and looking at me. I think they're arter me, m'm. I get in bed the other side I do.'

'O.K., O.K., we'll do something about it.'

'Ooh thank you, madam. I dursent take me stockings off in case I find them grubs wiggling in me toes. So I go to bed in them too, m'm.'

Oh dear! It'll be things that go bump in the night next.

January 1954

Nevertheless, even with Ellen here, I do wonder why on earth I try to relax, especially during the holidays, but Rachel, my former art lecturer, has sent me the latest draft of her book on teaching art to children (for which my tribe are guinea-pigs) and I am revising it here in bed, the only place I can find peace. I have just got to a statement which says: 'Good taste in children is instinctive but it can be confused by ugly

79

surroundings and even lost altogether in adult life. One of the best opportunities a child can have is to grow up in a simple beautiful home...'

Oh yes?

Outside the bedroom door Roger is yelling, 'Whang, whang, *doyng'* and then something doyngs, very loudly. Nana is calling out that no child is to go out in the cold, 'because the wind will blow your head off', and two others come up to me for pocket money. I am getting a fourth by remote control to make her bed and have just settled an argument about biscuits by giving them one each out of a special Christmas box, a communal present, hidden away for special occasions. I consider this a very special occasion. Having out-Solomoned Solomon, I slide down the bed again and give my attention to the manuscript. But not for long...

Nicola and Penny, just off to the eye-clinic, and muffled against the wind, yell through the letter-box that they have locked themselves out and their pocket-money inside. Will someone please open the door? I find this extraordinary as our doors are never locked, but the two of them seem to be right. The letter-box rattling continues and no-one, except me, hears. Where the hell can they all be? Kitchen door firmly closed, lots of instructions going on behind it, I descend the stairs halfway and shout; more I will not do.

Returning upstairs, I yank Joanna away from the bathroom keyhole where she is giving a commentary on the others' ablutions. As I lie there simmering, I think of a way for the three littlest ones to use up their energies and earn some more pocket-money, so I call them together and make an offer: threepence each for finding Dad's trousers that need mending, and a penny for every four hankies collected for the wash. This sends everyone off immediately into the far corners of the house. Sue thrusts a head round the door and asks: 'Ha'penny for two?'

'Yes, ha'penny for two.' Silence, broken only by sounds of scurrying.

Eventually they bring their trophies. Sue found the trousers, Janet has the hankies, strangely enough because she is shortsighted. I pat her on the back, pay 'em all out and they disappear. But again not for long. Sue suddenly bursts in, outraged: 'Do you know what Janet did? She took the dirty hankies that were already in the laundry basket. That's not fair.' Well, I'm afraid life isn't fair and Janet has gone beyond reprimand. She has gifts I wotted not of.

Peace for almost an hour. I lie prone, imagining I can feel the cells renewing, yet knowing deep down that they darn' well aren't. Ellen brings up a cup of coffee. This is flirting with luxury. It is half-drunk when the door explodes open. There stand Penny and Nicola, back from the eye-clinic, where Nicola has taken Penny for the quarterly inspection. The sight of Penny in a bulging yellow mac, green hat back to front, glasses gleaming urgently and arms full of orange balloon, green trumpet and red book, would have made even Rachel waver.

I survey them calmly. 'Good taste in children is instinctive...' Can't the theory ever go wrong? Is there never a rogue cell somewhere? Better to return to the manuscript. Picking up the pencil, I push on. Ah, 'a simple beautiful home...'

February

We did eventually get Rachel's manuscript typed but I doubt whether it will ever get published as Rachel is temperamental with publishers, even though she has one series of 'How to Paint' books published and going merrily.

Rachel is involved in an eternal odyssey. Homeless and arthritic, she goes from friend to friend, seeking the ideal environment in which to work. As a last resort, she has gone to live with a reactionary colleague. Life is, she writes, grim. 'I miss the children and the brightness.' We missed Rachel too at first, but life does, hectically, go on.

News on the grandma front is not too good. Nana Loomes is slowly recovering from her gastritis and I have applied for Ellen to live in permanently, her probation period being at an end. Nana B. has been taken into hospital with an unspecified illness about which Deene is very reticent. We fear it could be cancer. I cannot ever connect Nana with any form of dissolution, she who is the embodiment of life and warmth, so we are all a little sober about it just now.

February 28th and Nanalou's 77th birthday

Joanna went to school at half-term. We missed her, Nana, Ellen and I, but she is now much too alert to be deprived of school. Each day on return she gives us a resume of school happenings.

The first day she ate up all her dinner and Rosie McMahon was naughty.

The second day the teacher read 'Teddy Robinson' to the class and Rosie was still naughty.

The third day Joanna fell down and Rosie was good. I felt a strong fellow-feeling for Rosie McMahon. Joanna seems to be blossoming at school; it suits her. One evening she burst in:

'Some of them in class get naughtier and naughtier, and some of us get gooder and gooder.'

'Is that so? And who are us?'

'Me and Margaret and Bernadette. And two others. That's five. And we did sums today.'

'What did you learn?'

'One and one is two, two and two are four, four and four is eight.'

'You don't know what makes ten,' jibes Penny, one year older and bright as a button.

'Yes I do, somefin' and somefin' make ten.' Joanna won't be beaten.

March

We now have a BUS BEHAVIOUR CHART because I hear the two littlest ones are misbehaving themselves on the buses. I suspect Joanna is the ringleader but Penny, for all her ha'porth of size, can be naughty on occasion and pull off the boys' caps and swop seats. I hear from the more sober members of the family that the two of them are a menace and the conductor has threatened to tell their mum.

The Behaviour Chart is the only method of remote control I can devise. If they have been good they get a tick, if bad a cross. Too many crosses means reduction of birthday presents. So we have a little conversation, Penny and I, with Joanna intervening.

Me: 'Have you behaved yourself today? Can I put a tick?'

Penny: 'Yes.'

Joanna: 'Nana was on the bus, so we couldn't change places, like we usually do.' Good old Nana.

Me: 'Would you have misbehaved if Nana hadn't been there?'

Silence. 'Yes.' Then Joanna asks truculently, 'How long does this go on?'

'Till after Easter.'

'What will you do after that?' pipes Penny.

'Knock it off your pocket-money.'

'How much?'

'Penny a time, I should think.'
'Oh!' You can almost hear the mental wheels go round. Click.
'Alright, I'll be good.'

Saturday Morning

Saturday morning in our family is the nicest part of the week. It has a character of its own, perhaps because all nine of us are released from the weekday disciplines. It seethes with activity from the beginning. As soon as breakfast is cleared we put on the meat pudding so that dinner at least is assured. The children meanwhile are making their beds, a job that is done with more than usual care on Saturdays because of the rule, 'No beds made, no pocket-money.' Even so, there are blacklegs. A favourite short cut is to pull the counter-pane over the wreckage and another is to tidy the bed and not the room. I am now equal to all these tricks.

At half-past nine I sit down at the dining room table and dole out the weekly pocket-money: a penny per year up to age twelve, and then two shillings. At fourteen they jump to four shillings and at sixteen to seven-and-sixpence! Money for jobs is of course extra; for instance, a penny a day for bringing in the milk, twopence a day for clearing meals and another tuppence for making the toast - enough to be rewarding without being indulgent, we hope.

When all the money has been given out, off go the young ones to the shops. The elder children are more sober and jingle the money in their pockets for a bit. Roger will hang around considering and throwing stones till 11 o'clock, then suddenly, peep-pee-ep, off he goes on his bike. Nicola is much concerned with rabbit food and lengths of wood for a hutch, and there is much totting up before she disappears. Janet, my prize shopper, comes up with a long blank sheet of paper and puts down my list for town. Her pocket-money gets spent in between buying the weekly load of fruit and vegetables on the market. Joanna hies herself to the shops round the corner, and Sue may go either way, near or far.

So for an hour there is peace, while I attend to beds and puddings, find out the delinquent bedmakers, deal with tradesmen and peel potatoes. About eleven the local shoppers trickle back, all demanding drinks and biscuits. I check the change and the goods, and unearth the biscuits from their hiding-place. By this time the neighbouring children are knocking at the door asking for their special pals to come out and play.

The rest of the morning, apart from chores, is spent in Mum checking on the older shoppers returning from all parts, praising the bargains, getting shirty about the mistakes and mulling over the surprise purchases, which might be anything from a goldfish to a hacksaw. Sometimes there is a small present tucked in for Ma and Pa, like a blood orange, 'Four a shilling, very sweet, the man says,' or a doughnut, ('Mind the cream, I had to lick some off,') or a dish-mop. But no-one feels like work any more and to persuade one of them to lay the table is like trying to salt the proverbial bird's tail.

By a quarter to one we all gather for lunch, drawn by the smell of steak and kidney. It is usually at this juncture that Janet returns. As we have no car, she is usually staggering under a load of vegetables, possibly fruit cake, and inevitably a budgie or a goldfish in a dangling jar, hooked on to her little finger with string. And of course the Present. She ferrets to the bottom of her enormous bag, scattering onions right and left. She produces a foam rubber sponge.

'For you. The man was selling them cheap,' she announces.

I thank her profusely, add it to the other sponges in the drawer and we all sit down to the meat pudding. Saturday morning is over.

June

The garden and house are once again full of little things - chickens under the hen, kittens under the cat, puppies next door; lawns full of daisies and bushes full of roses. House full of alarums and excursions, and three or four interviews in the past week over Ellen.

The birth of kittens in unexpected places is a usual happening with us. This time they were born in Nicola's bed and she came down to my bedroom in the middle of the night, distressed. James was away so I went up to the attic to investigate. One little black kitten and one corpse or placenta - I couldn't tell in the half-light - lay sprawling in the bed. We took them downstairs and I felt we must deal with them pretty drastically as we could only keep one and the mother looked as if she was going to produce a few more. It was three a.m. and I looked out of the back door for a flowerpot to upturn in the pail to drown it as humanely as possible. But Nana in her new surge of gardening enthusiasm had removed all the

84

flowerpots to put over her brussels sprouts, so in the end I knocked out a cyclamen and used that. Nicola's sheets and pyjamas I put in the washer and the cat very firmly in the kitchen cupboard on a piece of old blanket. I then found Nicola curled up in the eiderdown, re-sheeted her, made myself a hot drink and went back to bed.

By morning the cat had had five more. I drowned one, gulped, for it is something I loathe, rang up the R.S.P.C.A., got no answer, drowned another, had a cup of coffee to recuperate and decided to knock off.

The next day I faced great accusations of cruelty until I pointed out that we'd taken the most elaborate precautions to keep only a male cat in the first place until Nic brought in a stray female. Animals *do* sometimes have to be killed, I said pontifically, else how do you think your dinners arrive on the table?

'That's nothing to do with it,' retorted Roger. 'We don't eat cats.'

But before the arguments got too heated I managed to contact the R.S.P.C.A.

The tale of Ellen is another matter altogether. A certain Cecil has been looming large in her life. She meets him at her sister's on her day off, and there is usually some slap and tickle in which the sister's husband, Joe, occasionally joins. Eventually the goings-on were brought to a stop by the sister, who complained that things had reached the bedroom stage. ('I ran there, m'm, to get away from him,' says Ellen. 'She ran to the right place,' says Matron.) So Ellen's liberty is now curtailed by order of the hostel committee but at least she is still with us, and I am richer by one more experience though Ellen, I fear, is poorer.

June

To even things up, I've just had a fine day in London, perfect from the word go. Mick O'Connor was picking up his wife at Euston, she travelling back from Ireland. Would I like to come too? Would I not!

A lovely green morning it was, with the mist clearing and the may just out, the fields chockful of buttercups (I'm a sucker for buttercups), and at Newmarket, where we met a string of horses coming off the heath, every man in sight seemed in breeches, four feet high and bent in the legs. The horses, forelegs supple as willow wands, were by contrast superbly lofty, picking their aristocratic way across the road while all the traffic stopped, giving us the finest sight that morning.

85

We bowled into the capital by the Barnet by-pass and Mick dropped me off at Swiss Cottage underground.

I surfaced near Liberty's among the morning shoppers. Liberty's, which I hadn't seen for years, was tantalisingly full of Ascot frocks, rare china, brilliant silks and all the goodies that used to entice us before the war. The hat department hit me like champagne. Here were fringed cartwheels in black, scarlet and white; raffia flowerpots sporting broad bands of colour; coolie hats shading haughty models, and huge floppy ones that brought back the twenties. But the flower-shaped fantasies were a riot; here a one composed of white organdy petals with petalled parasol to match, and there a gaudy blackeyed-susan, designed to balance tremblingly on the head, it too with a parasol, yellow-petalled, black-bossed. Obviously all was geared to Ascot and the garden parties. Who would choose to live up among the turnips, I thought, with all this going on in Regent Street? But then who would have the money to buy them? Certainly not us.

I had to wrench myself away to find the Royal Watercolour Galleries, in Conduit Street, and, still mentally in the aura of Liberty's, stopped to adjust my pancake hat to the current horizontal angle before pushing through to the 'Observer' children's portrait exhibition.

The exhibition varied: the heavy oils, I felt, made the children unattractive. I don't see children like that. Perhaps they were all painted by men. Women have a sensitivity about these things, as did the impressionist Berthe Morisot. The bronzes also seemed too heavy a medium for such fresh young subjects. But upstairs, the exhibits were lighter; the pencils, the watercolours and the contes suited the child subjects better, though I couldn't help wondering, gazing at these sick and maladjusted children, what had happened to all the cod liver oil and orange juice allocated during the war. However the show did strengthen my resolution to start drawing the family again.

Once more into the Bond Street crowds and past the lovely shops (the Queen's shoemaker showing subtle green and champagne shoes), I followed, on a whim, two fashionable women into Fenwick's snack bar. Self-service! A new one on me. There, balancing a pink plastic tray, I pushed along the counter, to find at my elbow a girl with a single water-lily for a hat, stalk upwards, the petals enclosing her silky blonde hair. The lily, poised there upside down with no apparent means of support, was all of a piece with her youth and her beauty. What shining perception to wear a water-lily on your head!

So into Piccadilly, where by Green Park a ravishing young man hailed a taxi with his furled umbrella, in the confident manner of Francis Marshall's 'London West'. Blissful to be in London again.

But that was not the end. On the bus, as part of this incredible day, I found myself next to a soignée young woman (surely a model), well made up, middy skirt, jacket with scooped-out neck, raffia flowerpot, pencil umbrella and all. She got out at the Ritz. I should have liked to have linked her up with the perfect young man from Green Park. It would have made my day.

As it was I fantasised all the way home.

August 19th

After a flaming start the summer has deteriorated into rain. Through the school holidays this wet weather has gone on and on, and today I am thinking of autumn. It has even affected the children, so Roger, seeing a break in the clouds yesterday, asked if he might take the three little ones for a walk. It turned out to be an excursion, even an adventure.

The morning's rain was still on the grass when they left about two, and I went up to my niche in the attic and slept. At four I woke up with a start, unused to the quiet, and found Sue sole survivor, hugging the cat. Of Roger and the gang there was no sign. I said to myself that I'd make a cup of tea before I went to look for them, but tea drunk there was still no sign, even though I went out and searched our long road and the immediate side roads. A small anxiety began to nag gently at my innards. At five I left Sue and Nana, also well awake and off I went on my bike. It is extraordinary the fantasies one can conjure up in a crisis. Sue said they were going riverward where the larger meadows and I had visions of them pulling each other into the water as one tried to rescue the other from death by drowning; or of one of them being mashed to pulp by the local train that chugs its way across the water-meadows and the rest scattering for help. I heard the coroner saying, 'We take a very dim view of two grown-ups remaining fast asleep while four young children are sent out on their own.' This guilt feeling made me pedal very fast - very fast indeed - out of our long road into the main road, heart beating like a generator, mouth dry.

Pedalling up Eaton Hill I met them, a straggly, motley crew, very cheerful, sockless, somewhat sodden. They shouted, 'Here's Mummy,'

87

and I scooted over the road to them, relief flooding in. Then I took stock. Fred Karno's army wasn't the word. Janet was half-dressed, in Penny's yellow mac, halfway being as far as it would go. Penny herself was sitting cheerfully in the pushchair dressed only in a cardigan and underclothes despite the slight drizzle. She was clutching a minnow in her fist. 'It's lost its giblets,' explained Roger laconically. Joanna lagged behind looking as if she had been through a hedge backwards, which she probably had. They all talked at once. They'd been to see the trains at the meadow crossing; they'd been to the mill sluice; the field was boggy and they had sunk in up to here (Roger indicated his chest but I found subsequently it was his ankles) before they realised it. They had been fishing: Roger caught a minnow in an old tin on the end of a piece of elastic. 'The others swished them up my way,' he said, 'and I caught them in the tin. We only caught one actually. I put it in my pocket but its stomach came out, so the one sitting in the pushchair had to hold it.'

Roger had organised the outing, as I thought. He had given two sweets as a prize in a competition for finding a hidden penny, and a girl had given them some plums. Janet had a sandwich in her pocket which she offered to the horse for a nibble. He promptly ate the lot, and nearly ate Janet, according to the others. All their shoes and socks had got wet, so Roger made a bundle of them and stowed it inside his lumberjacket.

'We had to push Penny through a stream coming back,' said Roger casually, 'cos she couldn't walk.' But they were all quite happy. We piled two into the pushchair, one on the bike and had a race home. After that we washed pretty well everything they had on.

'It was a lovely adventure,' sighed Penny rapturously.

These cold bleak holidays are always taxing, calling on Mum's ingenuity to fill them. The garden has therefore for weeks seethed with children from round about, the prime plaything for a child, I suppose, being another child. After that I would put in close order a truck on wheels, water, a vessel to fill and empty, a bat and ball, and buckets and sand. For variation you could add rubbish to make a den, a tree with a rope for either a climb or a swing, and marbles and skipping-ropes. Way after those would come sophisticated toys.

Today there are ten children in the garden and the favourite plaything is an old pram chassis on wheels, piled up in turn with bricks, buckets of water and children. Sometimes they rush round with it empty just for the joy of running, up and down the hill, through the shrubbery and round the apple-tree, while Roger stands by with a stop-watch. It is the stop-watch that adds the piquancy, introducing a bit of competition. I suppose on anyone else's property but one's own it would be called hooliganism. Pity.

September
    Autumn is here again with its crisp mornings and long socks and the children back at school. Most of them have moved up one class, Sue two, and Roger a whole school to the Upper Junior. Joanna has learnt all about the Battle in Heaven, St. Michael, Lucifer and Hell, but has not yet decided which side she is on, being a rebel herself. After all, as Bruce Marshall in his book says, 'We know that Hell exists ... but we're not bound to believe there's anyone in it.'
Sue found that she was top of the class last term and thereby acquired half-a-crown from Father. Penny found she wasn't and sulked on the sofa. Roger lost his dinner tickets and got sent home to have his dinner here, which I thought quite good psychology on the part of the teacher.
    Joanna comes in with her usual I've-made-up-my-mind expression. 'I'm going to save up and buy you a Christmas present this year.'
    'Good. Where are you going to get your money from?'
    'From you. You give it to me and then I buy a present with it.'
    'Well, that will make a change from pinching it from my coat pocket.'
    'Penny's been telling tales on me.'
    'No. I just have eyes in the back of my head.'
    Silence.
    'Have you really got eyes in the back of your head? Can you see the ceiling then with your back eyes?'
    'No, not ceilings, only things that go wrong.'
    'What sort of people have back eyes?'
    'Mostly mothers.'
    Knots in tails, everywhere I go there are knots in tails. It all started with Brownies. Sue and Janet came home one night each sporting a cardboard mouse with a long string tail. Every time they did a good deed

they put a knot in the string. Janet had eleven in hers in quick succession; for whom she did the good deeds, no-one knows. Then Roger decided to improve on the racket and made an elephant for Penny.

'But elephants have tiny tails, Roger.'

'O.K. I'll make Penny a jet plane, they have enormous smoke tails.'

So he made jet planes, and they too acquired knots and there was feverish competition for a week. Then as suddenly as it all started, it ceased, and strings and good deeds were no more.

December

'Who'll come and see my big spot before I cover it up?'

Two more with chicken-pox. Heavens, what's the quarantine for chicken-pox? I should know: these are patients five and six.

✝   ✝   ✝

Here they go out into the blast again, Sue and Janet in their Brownie brown, Sue long-legged and pale after three and a half weeks of chicken-pox and impetigo, the impetigo having developed in the chicken-pox spots. Poor Sue. At one point we had to paint her with gentian violet, the general effect being rather like a purple Dalmatian. She is shorn of hair and a bit tearful generally, but we've polished her up to look nice for school, hair ribbons and Brownie tie being ironed in a hurry on the bedroom mat.

The two youngest have become angels in the school nativity play. Penny was an angel first and then somebody was ill (chicken-pox again, no doubt) so Joanna was made an angel too. Out of Nana's trunk we unearthed for her a long white shift with a round neck, worn by Great-Aunt Jane 'way back in 1910, and another with intricate tucking for Penny.

Joanna burst in one night after school: 'And I have to kneel down and cross my arms like this and SING.'

'And what do you sing?'

'A hymn called Angels-we-have-heard-in-heaven,' and she rattled through three verses of it. 'And Shaun O'Rafferty is Herod.'

90

'Oh he's my best boy friend,' said Penny archly, with a giggle. 'I'm going to marry him.'

'No you're not, 'cos I'm going to marry Shaun O'Rafferty, so there!'and she adds with more than a touch of malice, 'Penny looks silly up there on the platform with one bit of glasses up here and the other down there.' But Penny didn't care. She was chosen to be an angel and this was her moment.

The next time I fetched them from school a rehearsal was in progress, a semi-dress rehearsal it seemed from the assorted garments that hung about the children. Most of them were wearing only headdresses and a polyglot collection of scarves, dusters, tea-towels, tinsel crowns and burnouses. Below that the attire varied, such as coloured bath-robes or zip-up dressing gowns with a peppering of pyjamas and striped curtains tied round with sashes.

'Which are which?' I whispered hoarsely to my neighbour.

'Tea-towels and rugs are shepherds; dusters and dressing-gowns are People at the Inn. Roughly speaking.'

'And the tinsel-tops?'

'Angels.'

'But where are all the angels' gowns?' I croaked, thinking of all the laundering we'd done.

'Keeping clean for the Day.'

'Sh-sh,' hissed Joanna in front. 'We're going on.'

A dressing-gowned stage assistant brought on two large fruit skips, one painted brown and the other green, and piled them one on top of the other in the centre of the stage. Mary, accompanied by Joseph, tenderly bearing a baby doll wrapped up in a shawl, laid it reverently in the top crate. A tall pale lass with no headgear at all so that it was difficult to identify her, reared up behind the couple with a large fishing from which dangled a silver star just above Joseph's head.

And here came the angels, six of them, tinsel a-twinkling, arms crossed reverently, and the piano swung into 'Angels we have heard on high'. I had to admit that Penny wasn't exactly the prototype of an angel, though Joanna looked seraphic enough, which just goes to show how deceptive are appearances. But just then they were all called to task for having their backs to the audience.

'Angels, angels!' rapped Miss Russell, 'we don't want to see your backs and we do want to hear your voices. About turn.' So they about-turned and were immediately embarrassed at the phalanx of mums standing sentimentally at the back.

'I felt silly,' said Joanna afterwards.

'Not as silly as you looked,' ripped out Penny.

Then on came the tea-towel-and-rug brigade, headbands by now slipping, and checks and stripes somewhere around their ears. They too hovered round the manger, crooks in left hand (all noticeably like walking-sticks)' and sheep substitutes in right, ranging from mock-lamb pyjama cases to pandas and teddy bears, and with one accord the whole group bawled out:

'Erway in a manger
Er crib for er bed,
The littul Lord Jesus
Lay down His sweet head...'

What a male-orientated affair a nativity play is! There was only one woman and that was Mary, for although the angels were in flowing robes, who could say they were female? I saw schism ahead at the thought of it. For certain, Michael, Gabriel, Lucifer et al were all robustly male. However there are incipient signs of sex equality. Penny's pal Tessa was one of the Three Kings. I watched her tuck her fair hair up under her crown.

'So you're a Wise Man then?'

She looked at me gravely with her big blue eyes: 'Oh no. I'm a Wise Person. Teacher says.'

Well, well.

The hymn came to a cacophonic end. Herod and the Wise Persons were yet to come but Joanna and Penny were finished. Miss Russell admonished them all as they broke up: 'Angels' gowns are to be kept clean for the Play, tell your mothers.'

There came back to me the Bible reading that had introduced the play, 'Man looks at the outside, the Lord looks at the heart.' Surveying the collection of scarves, rugs, pyjamas and tea-towels, I felt sure the Lord was right.

92

December 13th

So Herod was King, Herod was King at last. We have seen the PLAY, we have marvelled at the angels. Penny, glasses straight for once, appeared at fleeting intervals behind Joseph, Courtiers, Shepherds and other fry. Joanna, in clean shift, one wing of hair caressing her left ear, knelt among the angels with her arms duly crossed. The nightgowns shone whiter than white, the Kings came resplendent in velvet and brocade; the People at the Inn jostled each other in rainbow cottons, and Herod stole the show with a startling black beard. There were, of course, snags: the Star fell off the fishing rod at the most reverent moment; one small angel, overcome at the sight of so many people looking at her, left a little puddle on the platform and was hustled off by a shepherd; and Miss Russell, bringing on the Village People in the wings, had suddenly to mop up after a page boy who had been sick all down the corridor. But we in front didn't know all that; we were enfolded gently in the tale of Bethlehem, its sounds lost in the high roof of a school converted from a church, its scenery dwarfed by the peeling plaster, and its music diminished by the maladroit playing of a school piano. But the spirit came over and I suppose that is all that mattered.

✝ ✝ ✝

Nana Barnard is indeed very ill. It seems to be a recurrence of the illness for which she was operated on some months ago and from which she seemed to recover well, but we're told septicaemia has set in. I wonder. James and I went down to Meadowfield to see her.

The pattern was the same as in her last illness, the fresh little sitting-room crowded with family who always rally round when anything is amiss. There was again the whispered advice, the guarded telephone calls, and always the inaccessibility of Nana, hedged around by the family's anguish. But then are we too not part of the hedge, each wanting Nana for ourselves, competing for the warmth of her attention? This time she is groggy indeed, her chest is inflamed and there are other sinister signs, like a lump under one arm. Deene called it cellulitis. I suppose any disease could be cellulitis.

Her fortitude is past belief. Only this last week she went in for a cookery competition for an old folks' dinner menu, and the local press had a large photo of her making a steak-and-kidney pudding, her hair tucked

93

under its usual net, a large white apron round her ample waist and on her face an expression of complete absorption. It had caught her in a typical attitude just as she used to make meat puddings throughout a dozen years, the only photograph I ever saw of Nana in action.

Nevertheless it had taken a hefty dose of brandy to get her there.

January 1955

Nana battled through for a month before the inflammation died down; eventually she was able to come up to Norwich for treatment. But although she was on her feet her eyes had lost their lustre, her personality its warmth. She looked dowsed. Something essential was missing, perhaps the will to live.

The next time James went down to Oulton Broad she had the same subdued air and moved about very little - trouble with her back, she said. The doctor seemed to know an uncanny lot about its vagaries and called it arthritis. Nana, with a diminished twinkle in her eye, just called it a bugger.

‡   ‡   ‡

March

Clinics

I seem to be spending most of my time at hospitals or clinics these days with one child or another for what are mostly preventive reasons. There are no dramatic developments in preventive medicine. The only time one's heart beats quicker on the hospital round is when one of the family has an accident, and this usually happens to the burstingly healthy ones who fall off trees or become targets for arrows. With Janet and Penny we plod along doggedly, adjusting, improving, realigning; eyes, cleft palate, teeth, legs, ears. I often think of Anne on these occasions. She identified with them as an extension of herself and suffered poignantly as a result. With me they are once removed; we are in it together, but they are not quite a part of me and I am able to be more objective. Perhaps it is just as well, for it is a long on-going battle that we and the doctors are engaged in, mostly quite bearable, always time-consuming, but not bloody enough to be traumatic. The traipsing to clinics is persistent and how mothers manage to go out to work and keep pace with the malfunctioning of a large family I simply do not know.

One year we paid twenty-four visits in three months; this last year a little less. This really does seem amazing considering that four of the six youngsters are in bursting good health, but perhaps that is why. Like the ancient Chinese who paid their doctors to keep them well, we in the Welfare State obviously visit the Clinic to keep ourselves healthy. At the time of writing Nicola goes to be immunised - two injections, two tests; Roger to be topped up, another four visits; and because a playmate slung a penknife into his knee when aiming at a tree, he goes back for that also. Janet goes weekly for speech therapy, and the three together for a tonic after illness. I don't complain.

At such times I pick up a dishevelled Roger from school, plaster his hair, wash his face at the school washbasins, pull up his socks, trek to the Clinic and take a place on the long hard bench outside the doctor's door. To sit here is as good as the pictures. The entire wall is decorated with posters, pictorial and otherwise, covering the lives of one's offspring from pre-cradle to grave. We sit and absorb them gravely. The first is spicy: 'If you itch when warm or in bed, you may have THIS burrowing into your skin.' Here follows an enlarged diagram of a fearful insect with six struggling legs. Scabies. We gape. We itch, but before we actually start to scratch our attention is diverted by a big poster saying, 'Trap the germs in your handkerchief or they may spread round the family,' and out of the mouth of a gent in the top right-hand corner goes a spiral of germs round the family and even the cat, bottom left. This one always  fascinates Roger, his head spirals with the germs until he reaches the end.

Our attention now is drawn hopefully to the next. 'Fresh air immunises your child against colds.' I look round at the fuggy room and its dispirited occupants and make a resolution to Open All Windows when we get home. We edge up the bench to the doctor's room. Here the notices become more personal. 'Mothers, book your midwife early...'

I think not, not until we've coped with the present six.

The door opens and we are ushered into a bright cheerful surgery, one half of a Georgian drawing-room, where once no doubt eighteenth-century ladies finicked at their needlework. I see their ghosts around. How far can a room deteriorate, I wonder, gazing at the chopped-off proportions, but once inside we get on with the business.

The doctor addresses me as Mother. I am always Mother when I am not Mrs Grant. Few realise my proper name; I suppose it is never on the cards. James and I sometimes laugh over this when I am relating the day's doings, for these doctors are his municipal colleagues. Being anonymous I can be indulgent over their little foibles, their occasional testiness and can even sympathise with their probing enquiries: 'How many infectious diseases has he had, Mother, and when, with actual dates, please?' If we have come for an injection we sit down opposite a comfortable bachelor doctor, well into middle-age, who has a kindly face and a box of chocolate drops in front of him. He has an Irish accent.

'Pull up his sleeve, Mother,' says he, and to the child, 'Now this will only hurt for a minute, just a prick and it's all over,' and he pops a chocolate drop into his mouth, pulls down the sleeve, says, 'Next, please,' to the nurse and we're out again with the posters and the fug before you can say Jack Robinson.

At these times my feelings are divided between the parties, the doctors and the doctored, and if I could be sure the children would not get diphtheria, TB, whooping-cough I would never put a needle near them, and for the needle-jabbing process itself I have nothing in re-commendation. Perhaps one day someone will invent a tablet.

April

We are still on the hospital circuit but this time with the grown-ups. Cousin Flo, Nana B's ebullient middle-aged niece, has gone into hospital 'for her legs'. They are a fearful sight, almost rotted from the calves to the toes and she is again installed, somewhat tearfully, in room 7, King Edward Ward, Norfolk and Norwich Hospital. I dash out on my bike into the steely afternoon to see her. Occasionally Nanalou does a stint for me and between us we have kept the visiting going for six weeks. Cousin Flo has few subjects of conversation, being in a private ward, but what she has are spicy. She is placed between the post mortems, the mortuary and the chapel.

We greet each other like long-lost friends, exchange pleasantries about the various delicacies I bring her and then get down to the nitty-gritty of gossip. First she explains exactly how, geographically, she is placed.

'You know the mortuary's down there, just below me, so I leave my door open to see a bit of life and watch them going past with the coffins. They do the bodies up beautifully,' says Flo, 'and lay them on purple velvet. Lovely they look and two porters carry them and there's always a nurse alone with 'em. I do wonder sometimes whether any of my friends in Ward 5 are going past, like Mrs Major. Oh you've had news about her, have you? Still hanging on, is she? Oh well, perhaps one of these days...

'Yes I'm really much better, though I still get shoots of pain. Ooh-ooh,' and she demonstrates lustily. 'But I don't want to go home before I'm really better, do I? I said to the Doctor, well there's no-one to look after me there and he said, 'Don't worry, we'll see you don't go out too soon. He *is* a lovely man. No, I'm not on a diet. No, he didn't say anything about getting down me weight. Don't want to lose me strength, do I? I've just been thinking, I've missed the Chapel Tea, that was a-Thursday, and the Institute Birthday Party that I should have been on the Committee of, and the Choir Social. But it's no good worrying, is it?'

I assure her that it is no good at all and that she is much better where she is in this bitter weather.

'We've got an old man in next door,' she bends to me confidentially. 'He makes such a clatter in the night, quite frightens me. I rang for Sister the other day. Seems he was fishing about trying to put on his trousers to go home, but Sister soon put him right and stopped him cussing at her. Awful swearing it was, I could hear it through the wall, 'cos it's not really a wall, you know, only a glass partition painted grey. Apparently it used to be painted only three-quarters of the way up before and the male patients used to stand on their beds and peep over, so the powers-that-be had it painted to the top. You would think you were safe in hospital, wouldn't you?' She chuckles. 'Well, I thought so but I'm not so sure now.'

I think somehow that she is.

July 5th

Here we go, Flo out of hospital, Nanalou in and sadly Nana B. still very ill at Meadowfield.

Nanalou's incarceration in hospital followed a period of extreme activity. Promptly with the threat of a rail strike she went north to friends. She had a stirring fortnight and came back several sizes larger than life, arguing cheerfully and powerfully with everyone. She returned in time for Norwich's Civic Week and sampled everything on tap, exhibitions, films, children's homes, bus tours and open days.

Then one night she got all the children to sign a big birthday card for Aunt Georgina. The youngest ones being in bed she braved the attic stairs, slipped, broke her thigh and is now also in the Norfolk and Norwich. At seventy-eight this is no joke and she showed great courage throughout the business of being taken to hospital and being X-rayed.

I go and sit by her bed with my shopping list and pencil and get my instructions. They are legion and very detailed and include more 'don't want thises' than 'want thats', but I take the list dutifully to the hospital shop and usually manage to get the right kind of fruit, fairly bland and nice and juicy but not apples because she can't bite them with her false teeth and not oranges because she can't bear 'em and not grapes because the pips get under her plate, so I compromise with William pears and bananas.

Sometimes I can't help contrasting the two matriarchs, having been over to Meadowfield again to see Nana B., quiet, dowsed, asking for nothing, complaining of nothing, seemingly glad to see us, just waiting for the end. Rightly or wrongly she feels she will be united with her John. But this contrast between the two grannies was always there and there is room in life for both. Nana Loomes is a Martha and Nana B. a Mary, though the dividing line is blurred. It seems to me that often Martha-ism is the practical application of Marianism. What then is the Marian quality? Perhaps an ability to listen to that inner voice, a serenity, a self-understanding. I ask myself these questions, having in mind the letter my old parish priest wrote me on my leaving Tyneside: 'I should like to see your plentitude of Martha combined with a modicum of Mary.'

Perhaps this ongoing journal of my Martha-like existence, written in the quiet periods at the end of the day, will be my sole modicum of Mary.

I am finding, however, as the outside world impinges more upon the inner that the quiet periods become rarer and exhaustion takes over more often. No more can it be a journal of day-to-day but rather of week-to-week, or, who knows, highlight to highlight, as the rites and celebrations repeat themselves and each child goes through the stages of the one before. It has been a journey of discovery, of myself and other people, a log-book. But the entries will, I can see, become rarer.

✝ ✝ ✝

July 14th

And today the chapter is ended and all the happy days that went with Nana B. She died this morning. Recalling them now is like looking back on days of perpetual summer. I think she generated her own sunshine. Vignettes of her keep popping up in the memory: Nana among the apple trees in the orchard hanging out clothes surrounded by a bevy of grandchildren, some proffering pegs, some pushing prams, several teasing the dog; or of her sitting in the sunny living-room with a baby on her lap, and although there was more of Nana's ampleness than actual lap the babies always stayed put, doddering and drooling cheerfully; of Nana marching Roger down the hall by one ear because he'd been cheeking her, her firm chin well in evidence; Nana without her dentures acting the giddy goat in the Christmas charades; or making jam at the Institute, pounds of jam, right through the war; or sitting with dog Mick at her knees, making him eat up his scraps and muttering to herself, 'I won't be beat by a dog.' Nor was she. Other times I recall her, hat slightly awry, just managing to catch the bus outside the bungalow where Cousin Flo was detailed to stop it, and though, as often as not, she only caught it by the skin of her teeth she never actually missed it. Yet looking back it seemed summer all the way.

Nana had not always encountered good times, nor were she and Grandpa John always established in the big house as she was when I first met her. In her early days she had been nursery governess in a stately home in Cheshire where John was footman. Florence then had charge of the youngest child, the son and heir, but also had responsibilities towards Miss Lettice, the eldest, and would accompany her and the family to London for the season, when an entire railway coach was booked to Euston. Once there Miss Lettice was passed over to her London maid.

Nana loved telling our own children tales of those days of luxury which, in the years of shortage, sounded like a fairy tale...

'The children had a dozen to fourteen of each item of underwear, vests, knickerbockers, petticoats, often edged with lace, and after laundering each one had to be put back to the bottom of the pile so that nothing was worn twice running. We didn't dare put a newly-washed garment on top. But sometimes we cheated; where a dress, for instance, had only been worn for an hour or two we'd iron it out, fold it neatly, and then put it back on top... So many gathers to iron, so many tucks to flatten...

And each evening the children, right up to Miss Lettice, when she was younger, would come down and say goodnight to their parents in the big drawing-room before being got ready for bed in their own apartments...'

Florence eventually married John the footman after keeping him waiting seven years. Even then Her Ladyship asked her very seriously whether she was doing right. But Florence was quite sure she was, stuck out that determined chin and went off to marry John, who had by then left service because of a weak heart and had started up as an open-air carrier in the Forest of Dean. His rise from there was meteoric. He went to London to learn the butchery trade and finally set up in business in Lowestoft. There in the house behind the shop where Florence helped him, they brought up five children and sent them to boarding-school, college and university. In later years John switched to trawler-fishing and when I first visited James's family it was to a large Victorian house near Lowestoft from which his father had supervised his last love, farming.

Florence cherished John and his weak heart for forty years and he died waiting to go into their retirement cottage. Then, heartbroken, she moved to a bungalow beside the old family home, and it is there, to Meadowfield, that all the family has trekked since.

Nana always sent her five children a birthday cake, whether they were at school or grown-up and away from home. When I first asked James (a post-Oxford graduate of twenty-five) to join us for a picnic on our punt, he said, 'Can I bring my cake?' and turned up with a large fancy tin, sent by post, containing a rich iced fruit cake, inscribed with flourishing letters 'Happy Birthday'. I was intrigued even then by the figure behind the cake.

The sun shone endlessly over Lowestoft the day Nana was buried and over the garden at Meadowfield with everything sweet-smelling and apple-pie and the hammock full of grandchildren. Just as she would have liked it.

† † †

September
Life goes on.
The last child has gone back to school after holidays that stretch back pleasantly into infinity. It's a lovely autumn, quiet, sunny and full of colour after a brilliant summer. Nana Loomes is entering her eleventh week of convalescence and has emerged successively from moods of impatience and despair to something like normality. Roger has moved up to the Senior School, an enormous school of seven or eight hundred boys, and his only complaint was that there was nowhere to hide. The children are lucky here in the garden in that there are plenty of places to hide, mostly our overgrown shrubbery euphemistically called the wood, which in spite of its shrubberiness has definite paths and fallen trees and some tall mock acacias and a striking red may. And there are three majestic walnut trees with good footholds once you're up past the first six feet. Roger, together with his current pal, Richard Crayshaw, has built dens in the trees, and there the more agile members shin up and hide away, and brew strange drinks and eat fallen apples and stolen raspberries. The treed area they call Maytown after the red may.

Roger is blossoming out and has started a newspaper, 'Maytown News'. He brought me a typewritten copy with a nonchalant air. 'You'd better have one 'cos you're rather concerned in it. It should be a ha'penny a read but I'll let you have it free.'

I read it with absorption.

September 1955

THE MAYTOWN NEWS

I have now started a new newspaper which will have all the news about fasions, the garden and advertisements. I hope you like it. If you have an advert. to put in it, you just write to me and I should be pleased to publish it. It will cost d per advertisement. That is all the news for now.

Editer
Roger Barnard

Victorian Pennies.

Apply Penny grant

Any-body wanting Blouses, Skirts, or Dresses made, Apply Sue. Cheap rates. Doll's clothes and Fluffy animals also made. Sue will also be opening a shop to sell these.

MAYTOWN

Maytown, the country in a garden, although it is not being used very much is still in existance. The main street, Archwood Street is not very clean but during the summer holidays it comes alive. The frontier is lined with bluebells, flowering currant and foxgloves. Our nearest town is the Faith Boulevard. A post is delivered three times a day and is properly stamped by the Postmaster and his assistant. If anyone is passing the Faith Boulevard you must post any letter you have in the post box outside the house. that is all the Maytown news for now, more in next month's issue.

JOKES

Teacher. What is wrong with the sentence 'The train arrived late on platform 2.?'

Boy. The train should be on the rails not the platform.

ADVERTISEMENTS

Wanted Urgently!

Pictures of Adam Faith, also Joanna will sell swets and old toys.

NOTICES

Mummy sayes will everybody be careful not to spill fat on the gas stove and clean out the bath after useing it.

Nana sayes will everyone always take their clothes when they have been ironed.

Daddy has lost his pipe so will any one finding it please take it to him as soon as possibly. May be a reward for finding it.

ADS ADS ADS

Lost: One white bike pump. Reward to finder. Roger.

Wonderful bargain Marbles 6 a penny. Apply R. Crayshaw

Anyone found picking apples of trees will be reported to Father. This means you-and you-and
Y-O-U

Notices will be one penny except the Editers.

October

Round to walnut-time again. Everyone, even Penny who doesn't like hard work, helps with the walnut harvest. By the middle of October the gales have usually brought the nuts thundering down, though sometimes we may have to throw sticks up into the tree to dislodge them. Remember the jingle?

'A woman, a dog and a walnut tree
The more you beat 'em the better they'll be.'

But during the autumn gales the nuts will fall down anyway - splat! - and burst their squashy black husks in the grass, revealing the light brown shell. Inside this again is the real walnut. And, my word, doesn't the rotten black husk stain our hands and our shoes and subsequently the kitchen. Years ago, when gypsies were supposed to steal children they used to rub on their faces this virulent stuff which only disappears naturally by wearing off. For the first year at Eaton End we all went round with what looked like tobacco-stained fingers until we found a method of protecting ourselves.

In spite of the haphazard nut-picking towards the end of October the crop really must be harvested before the November damp. So we collect the family together with rakes, shovels, tongs and assorted old gloves. Fallen walnuts, like the tennis balls, hide all over the place, in flowerbeds, bushes, long grass, and can stay there for years so that you may find a little walnut sapling three or four years later.

Quite little treasures, these. Birds too attack the nuts on the trees and I've watched a ragged rook peck busily at a nut until he had gone through husk and shell, only to lose it out of his beak at the last minute.

The family need some encouragement over nut-gathering, for it's a cold and backbreaking job and you can lose your spectacles as well as your patience, so I go out with hot drinks and we all sit among the soggy leaves and imbibe.

Keeping the walnuts is quite a problem as the shells go mouldy outside, our October sun being too weak to dry them out. We tried several methods like putting them on wire trays in the airing cupboard, but in desperation one year I wrote to the daily press asking for a recipe to do the job properly. Promptly came a postcard saying pithily in large letters, 'Sawdust, Mrs Barnard, sawdust!' What the writer didn't say was that the sawdust must be kept in a dry place; we put ours in an outhouse and they sprouted.

Lastly near Christmas, when I want them for cake-making, comes the shelling. By promising that they can eat as many as they like, I get Janet, Penny and Sue to sit in a row with a cardboard box between them, cracking away all evening. These three in particular seem to find it soothing.

But this is not all. On July 18th each year we pickle many of the green nuts before the hard centre forms, after first pricking them to let the salt brine in. (They look like large green olives and finish looking like large black ones.) They are then put in this strong brine for nine days, its being changed every third day, and on the ninth I spread them out in the sun for another three till they turn black. Lastly they are popped into jars and covered with pickling vinegar.

'What a palaver,' says James, 'heaven knows what they're doing to our insides,' but we all have a lovely self-satisfied feeling around Christmas spiking black walnuts out of the jars to eat with the cold turkey.

November 5th

Firework Day and the inevitable fog. In our family we move inexorably through the year's cycle saving up for one event or another, mostly birthdays, but in October it is fireworks. Week by week the children buy a few crackers, a Roman candle or two, a Catherine wheel, and Roger and Dad collect all the fallen branches in Maytown and build a huge bonfire at the bottom of the garden. Invariably too we get children coming round in late October with the usual scarecrow in the usual dilapidated pram begging for pennies for the guy. However youth goes so quickly that I feel some of it might as well go up in smoke and I divert some of our firework money to them. In another three years or so none of ours will care tuppence about Guy Fawkes' night. But now we push on with the ritual; the neighbours' kiddies bring boxes of fireworks and we provide the space, the carefree attitude and the eats, and all goes with a crackle. There were eighteen of us this year including two cousins who hung turnip lanterns either side of the gate where they doddered like a couple of grimacing skulls, their flickering candle-grins mocking the passers-by.

At dusk we all congregate at the far end of the garden, where Catherine wheels are tied to sticks and the Roman candles firmly anchored. James takes charge and lights the fireworks. The facial expressions of the children, glowing and fading in the firelight, are to me the most intriguing feature of the affair. The intense excitement of the little ones is a rare and transient thing that will not survive many more Novembers, and I enjoy its radiance far more than that of the bonfire. In fact, I am not a firework fan at all and I slink away after half an hour and put my feet up in the sitting-room, until the call comes for food. Then we bring out the doughnuts, hamburgers, baked potatoes or sausages and swill it all down with lemonade. This consumed at speed, they rush back to the inferno until the supply of explosives peters out, till the huge fire has flickered down and the final cracker jumped from between unwary feet.

This year Guy Fawkes' night presented us with a few problems. Nicola came into the lounge with her veterinary encyclopaedia in her hand. 'It says in my book that all animals should be protected from sudden noises, especially,' she added darkly, 'the guinea-pigs.'

I wished that someone would give advice on removing mothers from sudden noises too, but mothers, I gather, are hardly worth preserving.

'Supposing we do protect them, where are we going to stow all these animals?' I reckoned by now we had nine rabbits, a guinea-pig, a mouse, William the cat, and the fish and feather brigade, consisting of three hens, a budgie and a goldfish. We thought the last few could look after themselves. Care with a capital 'C' was to be concentrated on the others.

For the next day or so I heard no more and concluded that arrangements were being made at low level. As dusk fell on Firework Night, an evacuation of animals trundled past the window, plus children and hutches galore.

It reminded me somewhat of the retreat from Moscow. A second contingent of youngsters was finishing building the bonfire. Rockets were already lashed to sticks. The lemonade and doughnuts were stacked in the kitchen. I surveyed all these preparations with much satisfaction and reckoned on an hour's peace in front of the fire, as you may have gathered. No sooner had I put my feet up than in came Sue, maternally soft, her great buck rabbit in her arms.

'Where can I put Bundy? I can't leave him in the garden. He'll be frightened.' As the garden covered almost an acre I thought this an overstatement, but Sue was obviously very concerned and, after all, the other rabbits were being ministered to. I suggested the air-raid shelter. This horrified Sue. That which protected human being from bombs was in her eyes inadequate for rabbits. 'It's *wet*,' she objected, 'and dark and dirty. He'll have to go somewhere in the house.' There was a strained silence, but it became obvious from the pleading look in Sue's eyes that she had made up her mind where he would go: her bedroom, the little one over the stairs! Desperately I agreed, on condition, ON CONDITION, that she penned it in on the lino.

'Yes, Mummy, yes.' That problem solved, peace came dropping slow. Very slow.

The drawing-room door opened again. Old Woolly Rug, comatose in the arms of Janet; Woolly Rug who wouldn't know a firework from a cork popping.

'Why hasn't he gone with the other rabbits?'

'There aren't enough hutches. They'd fight with him. And he'll be frightened where he is...'

Frightened! He was four years old, half-blind and mostly comatose but ... oh well!

'I haven't a single thing left to put him in, so do think of something with wire netting on that we can use.' Wire netting. We ticked off various possibilities. Meat cover, too small. Fireguard, long since gone. DISHWASHER! The old American washing machine which alternated as a dishwasher by changing drums. The dishwashing drum was large, lightweight, with a central pillar and removable wire floor. I heaved myself up, unearthed it from the airing cupboard and placed it on a newspaper with the wire floor as a roof. We arranged that Rug could lollop around the central pillar, keeping his feet warm on the paper, and we threw him a lettuce leaf to keep him happy. So Janet, appeased, trotted off to see the fireworks.

Up went my feet again and this time I got my modicum of peace. Until I decided to have a look in Sue's room. There was Bundy reclining on the silk coverlet, quite oblivious of the little pen Sue had made in the corner. All that was left in the pen was what looked like a fur-edged slipper, which I picked up. I shall never learn, but this time the fireworks drowned my shriek. Four tiny teeth met in my finger. This was no slipper, it was the guinea-pig.

What's so special about animals? Why doesn't someone write a fat book on how to protect human beings?

I may well ask myself. We seem to acquire animals the way other people do infectious diseases; they just happen to us. People stand on our doorstep with animals in their arms and frantic looks in their eyes and say their mothers won't let them keep the rabbits/cats/guinea-pigs because they are dirty/noisy/neurotic, and will we have them? (I sometimes think we acquire people the same way.) Occasionally our animals just arrive, like the stray cats, or the duck that escaped from the market float and simply walked into our garden. At least that is the tale Nicola told us but I rather think she made foster-mother noises at it and no creature could resist that. Our menagerie has not been unusual but varied, and has included budgies, goldfish and rabbits, guinea-pigs, tortoises and hedgehogs, and I had to be very firm once about a donkey. I was rather sorry about this; a donkey would have been an exotic acquisition, but our garden is heavily cultivated except for the tennis court and who wants a donkey on that, to say nothing of feeding and fencing it generally. In addition to these various mammals, countless injured wild birds have been nursed to life or death by the kitchen stove.

Nicola is really breeder-in-chief and general factotum though rather a nervous one. She is constantly anticipating trouble and is much helped by the aforesaid fat book about animals which lists the symptoms of rabies, or scours or hard-pad or cat-flu', and seven times out of ten I notice they get it. I'm sure she wishes it on them, so that they don't really have a chance. Or else she says they might become neurotic, through in-breeding, just like the European Royals.

Apart from this she seems the only person in the district who can't make rabbits breed. Certainly we did have one litter from a borrowed buck, but after that there was a stalemate: the doe couldn't possibly breed with any of her own family because of the dire consequences, haemophilia or madness according to Nic.

A friend helped Nicola out by giving her the moth-eaten buck, Old Woolly Rug, but the doe scrabbled straw in his face and refused to co-operate, so the breeding was stymied again. Then one of her sons by a previous marriage was popped in by mistake, and this worked the miracle. A litter arrived; whether haemophilic or mad remains to be seen.

December

From now on it is Christmas all the way. We have moved on from the Santa Claus stage and the children now save their own money to buy for other people. This they have done since the autumn because by early December Father doubles whatever they have saved. By fair means or foul they have all managed to scrape some money together.

The passion for saving became so great that it teetered on the edge of avarice. Coins were counted at every turn, three times a day. As the hoard grew bigger it was washed in detergent, polished with Silvo, and at length, weighed. This made me put my foot down. I felt we were perilously near worshipping the Copper Calf; thus I decreed that anyone found counting money publicly after this would have it confiscated. So it went on privately, in bedrooms. I could hear its muffled clink. Eventually they decided that the clatter of their various tins was giving the game away and resorted to cardboard spice drums. Penny alone had a proper tin money-box in the shape of a telephone kiosk and decided to keep her Christmas savings in that.

One afternoon when I came back from shopping they all met me at the door in great dudgeon.

'Penny's taken all our money and put it in her tin and we can't get it out.'

Too true. We hauled the offender up before her peers. We announced that we should have to break open her new money-box to give everyone back their proper dues. With great solemnity (for these occasions must be formal, just like a court of law) I wielded a tin-opener and out came a shower of coins. Allotting it fairly was difficult, everyone claiming a handful as their own. Roger, for instance, reckoned he'd had two sixpences from Aunt Edith, plus one I'd owed him, plus 'some pocket-money and a few odds and ends'. I was dealing, I found, with the vague, the doubtful, the precise, the resentful and the downright unscrupulous and it took the judgment of Solomon once again to sort it all out. But eventually sort it out we did, and returned the money to the respective drums. This left Penny with two sixpences, a penny, a halfpenny, and a cardboard half-crown. The saving, thus rudely interrupted, then continued. Sue decided to collect old woollens to send to Yorkshire for a shilling a pound. So for a while nothing was safe. Father's old vest and

Roger's bedsocks were appropriated and there was a rare old argument about the bedsocks. Roger said they were to be weighed and he was to have a share of the shilling. We obviously have a businessman in the making there.

Their different ways of raising money suit their various characters, the two most obvious being earning through extra jobs, and the next easiest saving out of pocket-money, but these methods are deadly hard for some of them, to wit the Lazy and the Big Spenders. I forbear to say who comes in which category.

Anyway we finished the Savings Stakes with one tremendous clatter as Dad doubled the lot. This year Nic and Roger had scraped together nearly 10/- each, Sue 7/-, Janet 4/-, Joanna 3/2d and Penny 2/3d, and I don't think Penny would even have amassed that much if she hadn't earned sixpence for losing a tooth and a shilling for bringing in the milk. Work is not in her line.

Then came the longed-for event, the spending of it. For the younger ones there were two sources of cheap presents, a League of Pity fair run by the Smith children up the road, and Woolworth's. They started off first at the fair (only one stall) and finally I took them off to town, where we spent four hours jammed tight in Woolworth's, trying to spend it in a fair and proper manner; after which I put them on the bus home and hied myself up to the Flemish Still Life exhibition at the Castle. I found the pictures of grapes, moribund chickens and passion flowers soothing after the passion of Woolworth's.

Nevertheless the care and skill with which the youngsters had chosen presents was an eye-opener. Nicola, as usual, spent all her allowance on one or two expensive ones, and had to be subsidised, but she had chosen good books for Penny and Jo, a decent leather wallet for Cousin Flo and an india-rubber and two B pencils for me. Joanna had had a field day at the League of Pity stall and came up with a tiny bottle of lavender water ('only thruppence'), a Father-Christmas-shaped soap for Dad, and a comb in a case for Nicola, all carefully inscribed 'Mum from Jona' or 'Nikla from Jona' in spidery letters among the holly. She wrapped them up in her two sheets of Christmas paper and even had some over to lend the others.

Roger also chose well, a tea-strainer and a butter-curler for me (not that we curl much butter for nine), an oil-can for Dad, and bathsalts for Nana; and Sue chose pretty well too in her gentle and mature way, starting with a school-made traycloth in some stuff called Binca. I wondered, turning it over thoughtfully in my hand, how many of these precious home-made objects I have tucked away, embellished with folksy patterns and nursery rhymes and alphabets, and slightly loopy blanket-stitch. How many indeed still decorate the dressing-table and protect the windowsills under flowerpot-saucers? How many yards of that mysterious Binca have I bought, pristine and unsullied, to have it returned next birthday covered with patterns and fringed edges. I love them all, duchesse sets and traycloths alike, but I do wish the embroidery wouldn't shrink in the wash and turn the things into grey cockleshells, and finally into floor-cloths. It breaks my heart to see 'Happy Christmas' shining through a grubby floor-cloth on its way to its last resting-place, but who can say it has not had an honourable life? Not many people have 'Happy Christmas' inscribed on their floor-cloths.

But Janet was probably the sharpest manipulator, having bought some good cheap cards from a shop round the corner from school and given them to the entire class, who in turn obediently gave her one each back. The top of the bookcase was therefore covered completely with Janet's cards. Popularity means a lot to Janet.

January 1956

Christmas materially gets better and better. Early in December came two huge parcels from Geoff, now in Singapore. Diving into one of them, we found a dozen Chinese tea bowls, jade green, each with its own China spoon, and in the other some real stunners for the children, five frothy nylon dresses, pink, blue, lemon, turquoise and white, each exactly the right size and each with a matching brocade evening bag. When the girls put them on and twirled in with their Chinese umbrellas they looked like a ballet class from Degas. They also brought a whiff of that mysterious exotic world out there, where Geoff is building skyscrapers for the Singapore Improvement Trust.

Roger wasn't forgotten either. As befitted a sober adolescent he had from Geoff a deep blue silk dressing-gown with a dragon on it.

And James has passed his driving test so all we need now is a car.

✝ ✝ ✝

Alterations

I was much too engrossed with Christmas to record the building alterations which have been going on for some time. In fact today beginneth the fifth week of the invasion. On December 13th last benign Mr Walter, the builder's manager, appeared at the back door and introduced two men, Ray with the Beret and Mr Mann the foreman (otherwise Deafy). And, of course, himself. Slowly and paternally he went through the plans and the house. There was work to be done on three floors; a small closet with washbasin was to be conjured out of the airing cupboard on the attic floor. The airing facilities were to be brought down to the kitchen, thus saving us two sets of stairs to climb every time we aired the clothes.

On the first storey, the bathroom was to be rejuvenated, the bowl having cracked and the toilet having overflowed. Also the bath needed replacing.

On the ground floor there were several changes. The pantry was to be taken out of the cramped scullery and put somewhere else, an extra sink put in, and a little window carved out of the kitchen to overlook our sunny courtyard, where the children play. In other words, we wanted more room and more light, so the most exciting addition of all was to be a sun-room made out of the vinery. It is extraordinary, but in that rambling Edwardian seven-bedroomed house with nearly an acre of garden, only two narrowish slitty windows gaze on to the garden. I wondered what kind of character the original owner was; he couldn't have sat in the conservatory because it was over-canopied with grape vines and smelt of bulls' blood, except in the spring, when it was suffused with the most exquisite perfume of grape blossom, like muscatel wine. We should like to have kept it as a vinery, but what with the heating necessary, and the weekly dose of bulls' blood, and scraping the main stems and dosing them with gishurst, and the darkness at noon that shrouded the sitting-room, we decided against it. But I digress. It was solemnly arranged with Mr Walter (I thought) that the process of demolition and rebuilding should take place room by room; and that as we were forced out of one room we should have access to another. Having arranged this, Mr Walter clinched the matter by saying in his slow deliberate fashion, 'Will tomorrow morning suit you, Mrs Barnard?' After eighteen months of plans and waiting this seemed heaven.

'Tomorrow will be fine.'

'I'd like to start on the scullery, then you can have it to work in again.'

'Ideal.'

So they moved in, at eight o'clock the next morning in the week before Christmas. Now, five weeks later, they are still in the scullery. True, it has one layer of roof on and a tarpaulin that leaks; true the pantry has been knocked down and attached elsewhere; certainly a window hole has been knocked through to the courtyard, but it is *not* yet a scullery again; it is a wet, muddy, plasterless, lightless, half-roofed shell, on which a broken gutter pours merrily. In addition to which, James spent Christmas crawling over the roof-joints outside rearranging the tarpaulin so that the rain didn't cascade down our necks.

The one thing that *is* working (though still unfinished) is the top-storey lavatory made out of the clothes cupboard. Another finished bit is the middle-storey lavatory, though the day they finished that they removed the bath on to the landing. Now we sit on the throne rather like Job in the midst of the desolation of pipe joints, solder, stopcocks, spanners, pincers, cardboard boxes, snakes of flex and worms of piping, plus the plumber's working jacket, to say nothing of nails, putty, toothpaste and brushes, and a roll of lavatory paper dissociated from its holder.

I try to remember the worst day. Was it the day the scullery roof was being joisted and two gas men and two electricians arrived to work in it too? I opened the door from the kitchen to be met by clouds of brick dust, holes in the floor, flex looping like lianas from one wall to the other; eight men all working in and out of each other's legs, a gap where the new window should be and chunks of plaster falling on everyone's head. I promptly shut the door again, although it was vital that I reach the sink.

Or was the worst day yesterday when we hoped we were getting straight and the electricians arrived once more, took up the entire floorboarding on the first landing, and all the furniture and carpets from two bedrooms and dumped them on the cream carpet in our bedroom?

Or was it the day we lost both water *and* fire and that night had to use chamberpots all over the house and, worse still, run the gauntlet to empty them in the outside lavatory before eight o'clock in the morning?

Or even today, when with sleet driving outside, the carpenter invaded even the kitchen? This was my bastion; Mr Walter had promised I should always have somewhere to operate. I watched Deafy decanting patty tins and icing syringes on the table with a fury born of despair, and retired inch by inch with the kitchen clobber into the dining-room.

Even the day before yesterday was baddish, reminiscent of Mr. Blandings and his Dream House. In the sharp nip of frost with the lawn grey-white, among the wreckage of glass in the roofless vinery, Ray found three tubular heaters, spanking hot, vainly heating an icy world. He tried - we all tried - to turn them off, but there seemed no main switch to apply to, until Ray finally found a way of disconnecting them altogether. We reckoned they might have been on for six years or more.

Also like Mr Blandings we found that putting right the mistakes of the workmen through issues that had not been made clear or sheer misinterpretations, was going to cost us extra. For instance the plumber fixed a pipe to exactly two inches off the ground that was supposed to empty into a garden tank. I pointed out that no tank was two inches high, and added that while he was altering it would he just turn it round the corner out of sight, as we didn't want to view the tank permanently from the meal-table. He produced various twisty joints and did so, but added sagely at the end, 'That'll all go on your bill, that will.' I am now very careful that every job is clearly defined at the beginning, but blow it, some detail always eludes me.

Every morning at eight the company arrives. First we hear the plumber's motorbike revving up the drive like a tocsin. We then leap out of bed, those of us who are not early worms. At 8.05 a discreet knock is heard on the bathroom door. Ellen. 'May the plumber come up, madam?' Not yet, not yet. Scurry, scurry, everyone jostling everyone else in an early morning coma, till eventually the last survivor scuttles from the bathroom, surrendering it to the plumber to juggle with his interminable pipes. One daring young plumber's assistant halfway up a ladder chanted blithely, 'O-oh we can't get up in the morning, we can't get up in the mo-or-ning...' but only Ellen knew who it was. Every morning at ten, the company retires to the hut, and there perched on trestles and timbers smokes its fags and discusses its union.

At eleven regularly, Ellen puts out six to ten mugs on a tray and pours out the tea. Each day she counts up the company: 'Now there's Mr Walter, and Ray, and Albert and Deafy and the plumber upstairs and today there's Mr Butcher down at the cabbages, but he have cucco, he do.' Sometimes I also help dispense.

'The plumber's on a ladder outside the second floor, madam,' says Ellen, 'so the best place to get him is outer the bathroom winder.' So I go up to the first floor bathroom, shoot up the window and look up to the next floor. A handful of brick dust falls into both eyes and the mug simultaneously. I bawl, 'Tea,' and put it on the window-sill, but a minute later the plumber suddenly appears from the stairs behind me. The window-sill is just a foot beyond his ladder, sideways, so he climbs down it two floors, goes in the front door, and walks up to the bathroom. Having drunk his tea, he thanks me, goes down two storeys and up again, outside. I can quite see the point about time being money, and promise myself to judge the distance better next time.

Deafy was truly deaf as a post. He spent a week in splendid isolation, sawing and hammering in the babies' room. You could go in and make a bed and he not notice. His supplies came in through a wide open window which kept the first floor nicely refrigerated and it took him nine days to make a large airing cupboard, single-minded and uninterrupted though he was. Deafy had a hearing aid somewhere. 'When he git into trouble he use that,' said Mr Walter. 'I don't know why he don't use it always. Perhaps it makes noises.' I could tell him the answer. He was like our deaf accountant friend up north who when tackled on this same subject snapped back, 'Batteries is expensive. Let the buggers shout.'

It is amazing to me how long it takes to get a supposed prefabricated roof on. Perhaps because it is not really prefabricated at all, but consists of several processes. We are now in the sixth week of working. First they knocked down the plaster ceiling, and removed the tiled roof. Then they built joists across the chasm and put bricks between each joist. Across that structure came some slabs of Weetabix-looking stuff, wood-wool, and then, 'That needs screeding,' says Mr Walter, and so they screeded it, which is covering it with concrete, I think. After the screeding they notify the roofing specialists, for no building firm now does its own roofing. The roofers take four days to arrive and then run in at a spanking pace, set up a pitch boiler, light a roaring fire and run over the roof like a lot of black devils pouring pitch over the screeding and adding Ruberoid roofing felt and lastly granite chips.

Then back comes Ray and nails Essex board under the roof, and lastly, slowly and leisurely, Albert covers ceiling and walls with a pink gypsum plaster. I say lastly, but there are still the decorators to come.

However, the sight of new wood arriving for shelves, like fresh-cut celery, sends up our spirits, for surely the end is in sight.

February 1st

Did I say the end? Surely the depths! Snow and ice and bitter winds. The supposed hot tank and three lavatory tanks are frozen at 2.30 in the afternoon. There are three men in the dining-room plastering holes in the wall; the contents of the entire china cupboard are laid out on the table covered with a sheet, like a corpse. Deafy, complaining that he's had to move his trestle 52 times, is back in the kitchen; Mr Walter, augmented by two electricians, is in the scullery, patiently emptying yet another cupboard and transferring its contents. The fire is out in the kitchen, the heat is off in the dining-room. The hot water's off everywhere. Nana and the two current invalids are huddled in the lounge surrounded by dining-room furniture.

The snow begins to fall again. Another frozen night. Roll on spring, summer, roll on holidays and sunlit strands.

March 8th

But every nightmare has its awakening. We have emerged into spring and space and cleanliness, and a cowslip yellow and green kitchen. Linos have been polished, shelves scoured, walls repapered. We have two sinks in the scullery and elsewhere three extra windows, three toilets and a sunroom. At last we overlook our own garden and bask in our own direct sunshine. But not without cost, oh heavens, not without cost! The catastrophes piled up to the end, the last one being the knocking-through of a door in the lounge wall the day before a cocktail party. The workmen got as far as piercing the hole when I put my foot down. 'I have thirty people coming on Friday, all arranged six months ago, and I will not, repeat not, have a door knocked through that wall till after Friday.'

'It will hold up the programme, Mrs Barnard. The men have finished everything else.'

'They can sit and twiddle their thumbs, Mr Walter, for all I care, but they are not knocking a hole through into the sunroom until Monday.'

The message went home this time, and we hung a picture over the bit already knocked out and had the party. A week later we walked through a new door in the wall into the sunroom.

‡ ‡ ‡

115

But there have been small heartbreaks. Ellen has gone and Gertie come. Ellen left last Friday, precipitately, as her year was up and according to the revised Habeas Corpus Act, nobody is allowed to detain her against her will. She was free to take a job in the wide wicked world and, like a shot, she did. Poor Ellen. Off she went on a cold spring evening to be a seamstress in Cox's clothing factory. She lasted exactly one day. 'Too much sittin' down,' said she, and on the Tuesday got another job, this time at the High School. Yesterday she turned up to tell us of her first day's work there, a little nostalgic, a little weepy, and I thought I detected a plea to return. 'You've bin like a mother and father to me.' But by that time the Grange had sent us Gertie; she was established in the little top attic and I could do nothing. There's no-one so dethroned as last week's major-domo, another hand doing the work, another voice admonishing the children.

Not that Gertie does admonish them; she grunts and grumbles into her duster at them instead. I cock an ear at this subterranean rumble and just about get the gist of it: 'I weren't never allowed to behave like this, I weren't.' 'They never wash their hands prop'ly, look at this towel.' She reminds me as near as dammit of Caliban and when I think of our happy (if hectic) days with Ellen I could cry.

May 8th

We are still surviving, but only just, with Gertie. I now have a pretty comprehensive picture of what she doesn't like in and around Eaton End. It is mostly the children and after that the food. She has actively indicated by look, word and gesture her dislike of anything from pickled walnuts to apricot jam, and from linen tea-towels to home-made whitening for windows.

And, oh dear, the children! 'They do what they like nowadays. I wasn't allowed to burn matches.' 'I was made to eat what was put before me.'

And so on to surfeit point.

When Gertie refused to deal with the messages I sent by the children, one day when I was in bed, I suggested that if it all worried her so much we'd better part. This, astonishingly, led to thirty-six hours' tears, a refusal to eat, a sore throat and headache and I had to put her to bed and cope myself. This seemed so fantastically illogical that I came to the conclusion that all the Grange girls, bar Ellen, who was in need of 'protection', are basically neurotic and really invalids and will collapse like punctured balloons if their way of life is incommoded. As stand-bys in a crisis they just don't exist and we had already been told they were unsuitable for dealing with young babies because of this. But for someone as outspoken as Gertie to crumple up like this was unbelievable. So I had a talk with her and in the end located the trouble as not wanting to return to the Grange. She had her own little room at the top of our house and all her belongings around her and was snug and secure. A promise that I would 'let the whole thing simmer' restored Gertie to normal.

June

We let it simmer, but Gertie has gone back to the hostel. A further row followed by resentment and sulks on Gertie's part finished off the uneasy truce. In some ways it was a pity because she had her good points; she was a fairly automatic worker, but she just could not help bursting out at the children. One weekend I was in the scullery with them helping to make a catapult when she burst in from the dining-room and stormed at us all: 'Why can't you do it outside - I'm not going to clear this mess up, mucking the place up. What a place to live in!'

It was the last remark that stung me most. I said tartly, 'You don't have to live in it, Gertie. I know someone who's dying to, if you don't want to.' (Though I was wrong. Ellen didn't come back to us even to say hallo. The wicked world had eventually proved too attractive.)

I went back to the hostel and had a talk with Matron and Mr Adnam and neither was surprised. In fact Mr Adnam, the rat, said he'd given her, mentally, three months. I wonder if he realised the wear and tear on the family concerned for three months. But then his job is the welfare of the girls not ours, and there was just a chance it might have worked. We arranged that she should leave on the Saturday in a week's time, and this I told Gertie. It was a quiet week. On the Friday night I asked if she wanted to take anything round in advance.

'What! Am I going? I didn't think I was going!' she burst out. So we started explaining all over again. It was almost too much for me and in the end I sent her round for Matron to do the sorting-out.

On the Saturday she and her pal, Millie, took several hours to remove her belongings. Gertie had dug herself in for life. I shut myself in the lower bedroom and tried to relax. The endless carrying of boxes down the stairs followed me into my dreams. Then suddenly about half-past three it ceased. I turned over and slept like a log.

117

After Gertie we got Gladys. I suppose Gladys was an improvement; she certainly was a thorough worker though very slow. When she spent an entire afternoon vacuum-cleaning a couple of rooms I tried diplomatically to investigate why. She was flashingly quick with the answer. 'I can't do the jobs properly in the time: you gotter do a job properly. Some people just scamp it. If you're not satisfied, madam, you'd better go and see Matron. Everyone else says I do the work well...' and so on for several minutes. I was speechless.

For the rest of her stay Gladys and I went our different ways. She never spoke and neither did I. Her work was basically good and she did get quicker, and at odd times we came near to a conversation. But in the end Gladys left. She went to live in somewhere and a fortnight later she had run away. Uncontrollable temper, said Matron.

Dottie'll-do-it followed Gladys, as different as chalk from cheese. She came while some of our friends were camping on the lawn in two very large tents after a wet holiday in Wales. Dottie, whom I needed badly as we were fifteen in the family that weekend, actually did very little, but every new job assigned to her was received with great gusto, and the catchword, 'Dottie'll-do-it - leave it to Dottie' soon spread round the family.

Dottie was only allocated for a week and accordingly left and by the end of October only a very dim Elsie remained like a ghost, in the afternoons. In Elsie we hit rockbottom. It was impossible to tell whether Elsie had done a particular job or not. One day I found her vacuuming one side of the dining-room floor, the other side still full of toys, lying around anyhow. I debated with myself for a full minute what could have happened. Had the toys been picked up and put down exactly as before or just not removed at all? In the end I asked. Elsie hung her head, bit her lip and confessed she 'hadn't got round to the other side yet'. I felt we had sucked dry the resources of the hostel. They had done their best by us and we by them. The next week I put an advert. in the Daily Press.

It was Marina from the village of Wymondham seven miles away who finally joined us. She slipped so quietly into our lives and fitted in so well that I almost forgot to record her coming.

In answer to my advert. a charming Danish girl had originally turned up. We bought a new mattress for the little corner attic bed where Gertie had bastioned herself so impregnably. But no sooner had we kitted up the room than Ingrid rang to say that six children was more than she felt she could cope with. I had to concede that I felt like that sometimes too.

But Marina (Rena to those who knew her well) had no such blockage. She answered my amended advert. one morning when I was out and Nana describing her said, 'She's another Ellen,' so we followed her up to a little cottage on the Wicklewood road nearly a mile from Wymondham, and fixed things up there and then. She would cycle each morning to Wymondham, park her bike and catch the bus in to Norwich. And did we want her to work Sundays? We looked at her stunned. *Would* she work Sundays? Yes, Sunday mornings she would. She was used to working Sunday morning at the hotel. So Rena of the modest mien, dark curly hair and gypsy earrings came to join us all at Eaton End, Sunday mornings and all.

July

Gabriella has entered our lives and with her the rudiments of the Italian language. Gabriella is what the Italians call 'simpatica', meaning that she is charming and makes you feel good when you really know you aren't. Gaby runs the evening class at the local Technical School and James and I, hoping to go to Italy one day, joined her class after a year of studying on our own. Gabriella is the epitome of all things Italian; she gives you credit for meaning well; she goes by the spirit, not the letter, the heart not the head. Precise facts like time-tables, marks, attendances are casually misted over in a cloud of good intentions. If James cannot turn up one evening she marks him 'present' in the register ('I know he would have come if he could'); if I don't give in my homework she writes down 90% ('Which is what you would have got if you had done it'), and if we muddle our tenses 'Buon accento' is the encouraging comment. We are all good scholars in her eyes and each week we return home kidding ourselves that we have the Italian vernacular rolling off our tongues when we know secretly that we can only just pass the time of day. Such is the ambience of Gabriella.

After a term of dallying pleasantly with Italian I got a telephone call from her. 'Would you,' she crooned down the receiver, 'be on the committee of an Anglo-Italian Society?' I cannot resist Gaby and I found myself saying yes and joining a dozen or so others drinking coffee and planning Anglo-Italian relations in Norwich. We knocked out a programme, booked a room, arranged a couple of slide films and assembled one night with pencils, paper and sixty chairs, the chairs being mainly for the Neapolitan girls from the clothing factory, and for any other enthusiasts who might turn up.

Looking back, one can only marvel at the thought of our welcoming outsiders. The Italians welcomed us; in fact they took us by storm. Bright black-haired Neapolitan girls, earrings jiggling, pattered in their high heels past the registration table, filled up the chairs, the window-sills and the floor. The secretary gave up coping with the accents and got them to write their own names, and the coffee organiser begged the management to double the number of cups. Such is the Italian sense of time that the flood continued for an hour, by which time the president had desperately made his speech and the committee were having an emergency meeting in the corridor. The film did create quiet for at least twenty minutes, but as soon as it was over ninety people besieged the coffee table, and the tumult continued.

In retrospect the first half was comparatively peaceful. The second film, on Alassio, set them off again. Every time the slides changed the undercurrent of conversation seethed. Like the buzzing of bees it added to the overheated temperature of the room and no organised activity was able to rise above it. So Gabriella jumped on the table and started them off on Neapolitan songs, incomprehensible to us, though the eye-flashing, hip-wiggling and applause of the natives gave us a pretty good clue. 'Very naughty,' whispered Gaby, when I asked the burden of the song, and pulled another hipwiggler on to the table, so that in no time the place was in an uproar.

After an hour of this most of the English staggered out into the fresh air, and I too turned for home, feeling that we missed quite a lot in Britain having no hipwiggling songs of our own.

Thus in such riotous circumstances the Societa Italo-Inglese was born.

‡   ‡   ‡

After the films, the dinner. It was inevitable that we should eventually get round to food and put on a genuine Italian meal, but when we started to thrash out a menu the confusion began. Now 'thrash out' seems a harsh word to describe a menu especially as we had already decided to have pasta, probably spaghetti, as one of the courses. But there is pasta *and* pasta; what mostly counts is the sauce. The Italian girls came from different regions and no two of them could agree on the classical way to cook spaghetti (or tagliatelle, or vermicelli or any of the others), for there is spaghetti Bolognese, Napolitana, Milanese, and even Piedmontese and Siciliana as I soon found out; to say nothing of pastas with anchovies, egg, bacon or onion, or even with meat balls and clam sauce.

But having agreed in the end that the first course would be ravioli, the escalopes of veal Milanese went through without a murmur, nor did anyone argue about the fresh fruit salad and coffee. All this, it was decided, was to take place at Eaton End.

On the day itself Gabriella and my pal Lynette, an expert cook, took over the kitchen from three in the afternoon until half-past eight (reinforced by many cups of coffee) for the chore of making a hundred-and-fifty-eight envelopes of ravioli, for though only fourteen people were actually coming the preparation seemed the same as for twenty. And accidents? Well, yes, we did empty the nutmeg drum into the mince so that the whole lot had to be washed out, which probably served us right for not using fresh nutmeg in the first place.

However nobody noticed this in the final triumphant presentation. Under the influence of the Asti, the red Chianti provided by James, to say nothing of Gabriella's food, we all mellowed nicely. I did feel, though, that if one of us had jumped on the table and sung Neapolitan songs it would have perfected the evening. But in these cold climes it seems you can't have everything.

September

Some time after the founding of the Societa, James and I travelled to Italy. At seven o'clock one sunny morning we were decanted at Milan Central Station, where in some place round its perimeter waited the autobus for Lake Garda. We looked round unsuccessfully for the coach stop. No sign of it. Well, it was no good dithering; we would have to make the supreme effort and ask in Italian. My sentence carefully rehearsed, I approached a man behind the bookstall: 'Dov'e la stazione di autobus, per favore?'

I expected a reply like 'Andare diritto', go straight on, or perhaps turn to the right or left, and for these I was prepared, but he simply said, 'Quale autobus?' Quale autobus? What sort of autobus was that? Suddenly nonplussed I panicked and turned to James.

'Autobus per Gardone,' boomed James.

'Ah, autobus per Gardone. Non so,' shrugged the bookstall keeper and turned away. He didn't know. So we showed our ticket to what seemed an official wearing a peaked cap, who looked at the small words, 'Cook's Wagon Lits', and said several times, 'Cook's Wagon Lits, sopra, sopra.' Sopra was up a long, long escalator. We put selves and luggage on it and were duly carried up. At the top of the stairs, Mr Cook's rep. jabbered in Italian and pointed downward, 'Sotto!' So down we went again, by now looking apprehensively at our watches. Peaked cap recognised us again, nodded his head at *his* watch and said, 'Dieci minuti,' ten minutes, but he took us down to the colonnaded entrance, pointed to some distant spot behind a car and behold, there was a bus stop. In five minutes a gleaming blue coach arrived announcing boldly on its front, 'Riva del Garda.' We were on our way.

I shall always connect two sounds with Italy, the click-click of the women's mules over the cobbles and the two-note horn of the autobuses echoing round the hills. I like to think that the mules were responsible for the women's upright stance and the provocative forward thrust of the bust. Surely one wouldn't be able to slummock along in mules as we Anglo-Saxons do in ordinary shoes. But I could be quite wrong; their stance might be something to do with their upbringing or their natural confidence or even from carrying things on their heads. I liked these muleshod women. The buses were another matter; they came round the mountains like monsters pursued by Furies and fluted like shepherds' pipes, only more aggressively, at every bend and tunnel in the Gardesana. Once inside one of them, a bus ride was pure entertainment, sitting high above the blue water, blaring through the villages, watching the lakesiders clamber in surrounded with their produce, fowls, fruit and warm brown loaves, arguing with the conductor, shouting at their bambini and climbing out again to the felicitations of their relatives. If you were to meet one of these leviathan coaches when walking on the road, you would literally take your life in your hands, which really reduced the issue to being killed in or out of the bus, according to taste.

Life centred between the lake and the Gardesana, the road that went round it. For the first week we sampled the lake, which in September sparkled like an English midsummer. It was reputed to be full of rose-coloured trout, a favourite of the Romans, and even the children fished for them with flat, square nets, or by dropping a line through the gratings in the promenade. The motorboats waited for customers at the Sign of the

Sail, and when this russet sail wasn't being used to attract customers it was cocked at an angle by the boatman to keep the sun off his lunch and his carafe of wine.

One enchanting day we took the batello and went to Limone under the towering hills and picked our way through cobbled passages under low arches, watched the fishermen making nets with red and blue nylon thread and the women slapping clothes on the flat stones by the lake. Here by the small jetty were shops gay with silk scarves from Como, jewellery from Florence, straw-work, leatherwork, and oranges and lemons from the groves above. As we wandered further into the village the magic died a little; the houses were primitive, in some places stone- or dirt-floored and housing both animals and firewood so that we weren't sure what was house and what was barn. But we came to realise this was a characteristic of Italy, and apart from the fact that humans looked out of some windows and animals out of others it gave quite an uncluttered look to the countryside. And how your Italian makes use of his vines! Those adjacent to the house were trained to make an arbour, an outdoor eating-place or even a garage simply by putting up four upright pillars, lacing them across with wires and training the vines along them.

Yet wandering below the lemon groves there came upon us the feeling of having seen it all before, the mountains, the lake and the long dark fingers of the cypresses puncturing the blue, and it was borne upon me that we were seeing again the Early Renaissance landscapes, spread out before us as they have been for Fra Angelico, in Fiesole, as fresh now as the day they were painted. Wherever we seemed to go artists had been there before us distilling the beauty into paint. Sometimes it was in the olive groves, also as old as the Romans, where the brittle grass was shorn to earth by sheep or goats and the sun silvered a million leaves; places so quiet and soporific they reminded me of Tennyson's Lotos-Eaters coming 'unto a land in which it seemed always afternoon...' This Italy was not the land I had envisaged of ochre buildings under a blazing sun, but a place where the sight of goats among the olives mingled with the flowers in the courtyards and the blue of the lake to create a kind of arcady. Idealistic, of course, for modernity was encroaching fast; already the stridency of the coach horns on the Gardesana was overwhelming the tinkle of goat bells and the click-click of the cicadas.

Nevertheless it was with reluctance I came back to cities, though James, in love with antiquity rather than flowers, insisted that scenery was just scenery, and olive groves just ideal places for siestas. Well, each to his own, but deep down I knew he was in love with the place as much as I was.

Returning to England at the edge of October with the leaves scuttling to meet us and the colour drained out of the garden, it seemed we had left another world the other side of the Alps. I suppose, like falling in love, it is the first savouring of an experience that stays in the memory.

Growing Up

March 1957

Six months on, in a passing year so full that the diary has taken second place to the urgency of the daily grind. And yet it has been in many ways a phoenix year; for the youngsters a time of subtle change, of new and strange desires arising out the ashes of the old, of borders being pushed out and burgeoning instincts reined in. Can it really be seven years since we came to Eaton End? We seemed to be leaving for good that happy haven of kiss-and-make-it-better, of Father Christmas, grazed knees and lost teeth, for the wider seas of grown-up-ness with all its uncertainties, euphoria and acne. This year Nicola will be fifteen and the youngest, Joanna, eight. Roger and Janet turn thirteen and below them Sue ten and Penny nine. Where, I wonder, have the years gone?

A rhetorical question. I know quite well where they have gone. In passionate entries in diaries for one thing. In straightening out teeth, correcting eyes and various therapies. In building up confidence and toning down tempers: in hearing Latin verbs and multiplication tables; in falling off bikes and throwing straight balls and not least in easing the transition from one school to another. The wonder is that any of us have remained sane at all. But of course we have and our most tenacious survivor is Janet.

At twelve Janet's pale silky hair is thickening into curls and in spite of the pebble-lensed glasses she has the makings of a pretty child. Her hearing-aid is a discreet little cream button attached to a battery box which fits under her pinafore dress. A casual observer would not notice it, nor the wedges that are attached to her shoes. This trip down to the appliance-makers with each pair of shoes is as much a part of life as the renewal of batteries, changing of spectacles and bracing of teeth; or the speech therapy and the six-monthly visit to the orthopaedic specialist. Just to make a change, the bone condition has been further diagnosed as multiple epiphyseal dysplasia, a fine distinction from the previous two diagnoses.

Janet's progress lately has been something of a switchback. She left the junior school at nine to go to the physically handicapped school round the corner, known to the locals as 'Colman Road Special', her deafness and shortsightedness not being bad enough to merit sending her to the full-scale deaf school twenty miles away. At Colman Road the pace was easy and she returned to the junior school after a year, much encouraged and fortified.

Janet's learning is still hit and miss. There are some facts she simply cannot retain, mostly abstract. Word-endings improperly heard result in some hilarious malapropisms. She writes letters in a kind of gibberish, repeating the few words she knows over and over again, probably showing a strong desire to communicate without the vocabulary to do it with. She still signs everything 'By Janet Grant', even shopping lists. This may also be the sign of a strong ego inhibited in most other ways. She is good with money, something she can understand and which buys her popularity. She is orderly, precise and fastidious.

Someone like Janet is necessary in a big family. She prevents us from getting too insensitive to the needs of others; she keeps us humble and our humour simple, and gives us an outlet for compassion, those of us who have it, and perhaps teaches it to those who haven't. Janet plays the equivalent, if she will pardon me for saying it, of the jester in the mediaeval court who was the antidote to the formality of kings. She is simple in the uncomplicated sense and we need her.

Penny, on the other hand, is as bright as her brown button eyes; she reads everything she can lay hands on, usually over the rim of her glasses which still perch precariously on the end of her round blob of a nose.

When I reported this to the school eye specialist he riposted somewhat frostily: 'This child cannot possibly read above her spectacles, mother: she cannot see.' Mother didn't argue in the face of such certainty and Penny went on pushing her glasses down and reading over the top.

She is slower than Janet in only one respect, her walking, because she walks on her heels and the rotation of the hip-ball in its socket is faulty. Recently the left leg was obviously becoming out of true, and she was operated on for a bone wedge, inserted in the outside of the leg to straighten it out. This seems to have been quite successful and so far neither child has had to resort to a splint nor, apart from Penny's operation, have they been kept in hospital.

In inverse proportion to her size is Penny's appetite for the blood-thirsty. She loves cowboys, war, space comics, vampires, hand-to-hand hand combats and mayhem. This may be a form of compensation because paradoxically she has tiny hands and feet and loves making tiny models, buying tiny things. Martial toys are the real stuff of life to Penny; guns, pistols and holsters, a suit of armour (plastic, 29/11 from Barkers), cowboy outfits, swords.

'How do you learn to be a fire-eater?' she asked me earnestly one day, thumbing a luridly-covered book featuring supermen being shot from cannon, and peppered with Zooms, Whams and Splats! That had me stumped. How *do* you learn to be a fire-eater?

'I don't know actually. Are you thinking of being one?'

'Possibly,' says Penny.

'Well, we could enquire at Chipperfield's circus next time they come.'

'Good idea! We'll do that,' and off she went, nose back in book, query satisfied. Penny always gives you credit for being helpful.

Sue and Penny are partners in crime. Playing Wild West with Joanna, the pair of them march into a pretend bar while Penny snaps out:

'Make it a whiskey, mate and make it fast!'

Wallop! Down it goes.

'What about another swig, eh Jo? Make it a double, mate!'

So they make it a double and wallop, down that goes too.

'Tha-at's better. Now we'll go and rob a bank,' says Penny rumbustiously fingering her holster. 'Come on, pard...' and the pair march purposefully off.

Sue at ten, with her wide smile, fresh face and thick auburn plaits goes quietly about her own business. I don't often record her doings because she is not usually being exasperating or demanding much physical attention. She has a quiet logic, which, young as she is, takes the heat out of situations and in her spare time you can find her cleaning out or cradling her precious rabbits. In our rather scatty family Sue, placed nicely in the middle, acts as the still heart of the storm. Next year she will be going up to the senior school.

April 10th

I thought it wouldn't be long. Sex is beginning to rear its problematic head. Nicola yesterday shattered the assembly at the dinner table by

127

asking, 'Mummy, have you ever been raped?' I looked into six pairs of enquiring eyes and knew that soon, very soon, though preferably not at mealtime, I must give an honest explanation.The simple no, like Patriotism, is not enough. Those who don't have family meals together miss a lot of sociology; there's something about togetherness, elbow to elbow, that gives one courage to challenge the mysteries of the universe. It took me back to another dinnertime, all those years ago, when I asked my flummoxed parents, 'Why don't people have babies before they're married?' My mother rallied gallantly with the reply, 'Shall we say it's not polite?' but with a twinkle in her eye as though there were more to come. But there never was, and that was the be-all and end-all of my sex education.

Well, the world has moved on since then and me with it, but here it goes nudging me again. I have been accepting smugly in my middle-aged innocence that the family knew all about procreation in its various stages because I've told them each time the opportunity came up and we've brought up enough kittens and rabbits for the rest to be demonstrably slotted in. But animals are not humans and I have been slightly unnerved lately by the experts telling us reproachfully that we should not only explain the whole business in the context of caring love, but that tenderness between parents should be shown on all adequate occasions.

So just now I am feeling anything but adequate. Are James and I giving off the right impressions? Is the time when we should be relaxing and saying nice things to each other, like early evening after work, being filled with hustling six children to bed? Has the Martha overtaken the Mary in the lives of us mothers?

I'm sure the experts are right (and it is a nice thought) but according to their tenets I must have had a deprived childhood. My farming Scots grandmother, for instance, had no truck with sex education or anything else being communicated gently. Arms akimbo she pontificated to her brood in a broad Scots tongue, 'Dinna dae as I dae, but dae as I say,' and by Jove they did; but then all the evidence on this subject was around them in byre and field, and in common parlance in the farm kitchens. My parents, in a softer milieu, were not so dogmatic but neither were they so forthcoming. One was supposed to know about coition by instinct though in blunt truth it depended on how much the girl in the next cubicle in the dorm at boarding-school knew about it all. The biology courses at college weren't much more enlightening. Unmarried women lecturers would deliver long spiels on scientific facts and go through experiments on the simpler forms of life while ducking the main issue. (Nothing below the chest!) We examined frogs (dead), we were referred to certain books in the library, but at twenty I started teaching in the east end of Newcastle without knowing how, or even where, exactly a baby was born.

Determined that my children should take it as a natural part of life, I soldier on, letting them feel the pre-baby kicking, and join in the birth of kittens, answering questions as they come up, in spite of Nicola saying that Mummy never told her anything, she'd learnt it in biology. Well, of course biology helps, a little explanation here, a little push there and eventually it all registers. Something at school evidently made it click and the click must take its time.

What made me think this way over the soapsuds on a sunny morning is that some of this has filtered down to Joanna. She has taken her dolls and cot out into the garden and is playing weddings. She runs to me across the lawn.

'I'm going to marry Rosella and Poodle. Do you think they'll suit each other?'

'Sure.'

'And will rose petals do for confetti?'

'Just the thing.'

So she trots off and marries them, and later comes back to report.

'I've put them together in the cot under the maytree. For their honeymoon. That's what people do, isn't it?'

I see Joanna has the message already.

One evening she had to draw a picture of Adam and Eve for homework.

'What did they wear?' she asked me.

'Well...nothing at all at first, but after the Fall from Paradise we think they wore fig-leaves.'

'I'll look in my school Bible,' said she, and there she found two tiny pictures on an illustrated capital, showing them both naked before a bush.

'I can't draw Eve like that,' jibbed Joanna.

'Well, put the bush in front of her if it worries you.'

But suddenly Penny piped up: 'You want to know what Eve wore? Nothing. She was bare.'

'Penny, you've got a bad mind. I can't draw her bare,' but I noticed later that with much crumpling of brow she had drawn Eve, top half only, rising from a bush. Conscience was salved.

There's an area of double-thinking here, and perhaps some sorting-out between decency and appreciation of the nude is overdue. Do my art school studies, for instance, cause moral schizophrenia? Because Joanna was brought up short at school one day when a teacher, defining modesty I would imagine, tried to explain why we don't all run around nude. Joanna, puzzled, had said, 'But my Mummy paints people with no clothes on.'

'That's different,' said teacher.

At home Joanna demanded, 'Why is it different?'

Ah why? I mulled it over, trying to put it in a nutshell, and concluded that it really depended first on whether the artist had intended the painting to be titillating, or not, but also on its interpretation in the mind of the viewer. Had she been a little more worldly-wise I might have argued that the normal nudity of, say, Papua, would evoke no reaction over there but would be construed quite differently over here, depending on one's culture. A complex issue, as old as the hills. Eve the apple-eater had a lot to answer for.

I tried to get this over to Joanna in an easy way, and decided that life was simpler, though not so interesting, when the issues were only measles and chicken-pox.

Roger, now, has no inhibitions. He lined up my life studies on the settee for a boy friend and with an expansive gesture said, 'Lavish yourself in these.' So the pair of them stood there and regarded the paintings in a fairly desultory fashion, grinned a bit, shifted their feet, said, 'Yes, well..that one's not bad...' They then nudged each other several times, bellowed with raucous laughter, suddenly lost interest and moved on to Meccano. To Roger they are part of the furniture and at least one throw-out, I hear, has finished up in the Corporation dust-cart garage as a dartboard. Perhaps this too may have psychological undertones.

April 16th

Nicola has had her long plaits cut off and is quite the young lady. She has decided to give up dancing classes because nobody danced, she said, With her, we imagine. Father suggested that she sat there and smiled instead of looking acid, so the next week she smiled. She came crashing in afterwards and exploded to James:

'Daddy, I'll never take your advice again!'

130

'Why? Didn't you get any partners?'

'Yes, I got a spotty boy who had nothing to say and kept asking me for dance after dance.'

'Well, isn't that what you wanted?'

'No. Yes, but not someone like that! Where are all the *nice* boys?'

James took his pipe out of his mouth and grinned. 'They're around. It's only a matter of time. The boy was probably nervous. Be patient and,' pointing the stem of his pipe at her, 'keep on being pleasant. You know the old saying, "You can catch more flies with a spoonful of honey..."'

'Oh Dad, that's awful old hat, and who wants flies anyway?'

In spite of boys Nicola's real love is horses. She has been planning for some time a riding weekend here at Eaton End. I realise that horses do fill a desperate need in Nicola's life but with six youngsters it is difficult to do much about it. The most she has achieved is occasional lessons at the stables down the road wearing secondhand jodhpurs and hat. But so great is her ponymania that I felt we ought to something towards it, so she and her two horsey-minded friends have decided to meet here and have two days' riding, Nic hiring a horse from the stables. Joy and Caroline, living in the county, will have long rides into Norwich, so we've planned tethering places in the garden and a night's lodging for the owners.

This involves more than meets the casual eye for we are no horse paddock. However we've tried. Joy's horse Rocky and the classy-looking hack that Nic has booked are to be installed in the old wooden garage at the bottom of the garden and Nicola has listed all the poisonous plants in the acre so as to find a clear patch for Gipsy, Caroline's horse. The most innocuous seems to be under the apple tree where nothing much takes root. We are surrounded by salt-lick, curry-combs, grooming brushes, hay, straw, ammonia smells and horsey talk.

So Joy and Caroline rode over respectively seven and eighteen miles from south Norfolk and yesterday all three went on the arranged itinerary taking with them a packed lunch. I had the impression that they were going to ride for miles along country lanes and come back for tea, but at midday, packed lunch notwithstanding, they all three turned up again.

Bewildered mum tried to find out why.

'We decided it was more comfortable to eat at home.'

Various sharp remarks trembled on my lips and died.

'So you'll be having your long ride this afternoon?'

'Probably.'

But they had no such intention. The afternoon was spent in sorties to the large City of Norwich boys' school. What a wonderful boost for one's ego to clop-clop along the main road and over to the playing fields of nearly a thousand boys. Much better at fifteen than commons and country lanes. Wish I'd had the opportunity myself, I thought nostalgically, but at that age, at weekends I was walking in crocodile in long black stockings, with two keen-eyed nuns at the back, and darting yearning glances at the odd choirboy pedalling his way down Brigg High Street. This showing-off operation used up most of the afternoon and then the three of them clopped back again, tethered their steeds and turned to frying themselves sausages and chips. Much later, after anxious examination of hooves and hair, the horses were bedded and the owners dossed for the night in the attics.

Next morning three euphoric equestriennes upped with the lark, tucked into three large breakfasts, took photographs of mounts and owners in various professional attitudes, and then clopped their way back to the country, leaving Nic to return Bracken. The photos however looked very Tatler-ish, taken between the drive and the ancient spreading walnut tree, and well away from the tumbledown shed. And Nic was in a dream the whole of the following week.

May

But events of a wider scope than horses are now upon us: the school party went to Rome for Easter. All my enthusiastic suggestions for foreign travel were systematically turned down, i.e. to lend her an Italian phrase book; to try a little wine of the country; to take some varied clothing as Easter can be both hot and cold. But there is nothing so funspoiling, I suppose, as someone who has done it before. First time abroad is like exploration into the unknown; it's one's own experience to be done in one's own way.

So Nicola had a good time in Rome and returned almost enthusiastic. Certainly the weather had not been too good. ('Too hot,' she told her history teacher; 'Quite cool,' she told us.) The convent food had been poor, especially the soup; 'Dishwater,' said she, 'with things floating in it.' The girls' and boys' schools had not been allowed to mix, but Diana Gatsby had got proposed to, somehow, and Nic admitted she had enjoyed

132

the whole tour, especially the mountains and the wild flowers and the lakes and the funny bits like the Italian frontier-man who ate a live squid for them.

'I saw it wriggling on his tongue,' she related, shivering delightedly at the memory.

But the significance of the Colosseum had passed her by; she photographed a small part of it with a boy balanced on its ancient stones, which, after all, was what it meant to her; and Castelgandolfo, that hallowed place, only provided her with a bottle of Frascati to bring home.

The party had also had an audience with the Pope, stayed a day at Aix-le-Bains and had dallied in Paris on the way home.

Comment of one who had seen four capitals by the time she was fifteen: 'All these big cities are alike; when you've seen one, you've seen the lot. Paris was just like Rome.'

'She's getting completely blasé,' I complained one day.

'She's growing up,' said James.

July

After sixteen years of marriage we have acquired a car, right in the middle of the petrol rationing due to the Suez crisis. James must have been one of the very few to have gained by that deplorable episode because the bottom dropped out of the car market and he bought it cheaply, an Austin. To celebrate we decided to go for a day in London under our own steam. I should like to record that we returned that way, but unfortunately no.

James has a tycoon's characteristics without being a tycoon: he spends

133

large sums comfortably and small sums with great difficulty so that it is like toothache to him regularly to keep on spending a pound or two. When petrol went up to six shillings a gallon and was in short supply withal he filled up his tank a gallon at a time and heaven help him if the journey took a gallon and a quarter because we then naturally stopped, wherever we were. In this manner, during this particular period, he stopped in the wilds of Suffolk; on the way to catch the 7.45 a.m. to Liverpool Street; en route to a dinner party; in most streets of the city and twice conveniently outside our own garage. From radiating points in the city and county came overalled men with little cans and funnels to fill up James's car, until eventually we decided to carry a can ourselves in the boot. So regular was the car in its emptying habits that it usually stopped at the entrance to the City Hall car park and had to be pushed in. It so happened that James's colleague, Ladds, cycled into the car park at the same time as Father and he would always prop up his bike and put a shoulder to the wheel, James's wheel, that is. The first time he did it with a will; the second time he said, 'Try putting petrol into it; cars go for miles with petrol!' but the third time he just said incredulously, 'No!'

But before relations got really strained rationing ceased. We therefore let ourselves go and planned this trip to London.

It was a perfect day: the car sped like a bird, the traffic was thin on the road. We reached the outskirts of London in what was record time according to everybody's estimates, parked at a suburban station and took the Tube in. Nor was there any flaw in the day's programme, a mixture of electronic computers and the Royal Academy. We dallied a bit at the afternoon rush hour to let the office traffic through and in the brilliant early evening sunshine set off for home.

'What a joy,' we said, 'to be our own masters,' as we smoothly ate up the miles, outspeeding great vans and heavy transport. 'What a civilised way of travelling after years of buses,' as we left behind a huge refrigerated meat lorry. 'We shall be home before dusk.' And then of course we stopped. The clutch waggled up and down uselessly like a loose tooth. With the remaining momentum James turned the car's nose into the last garage we were likely to meet for miles, switched off the engine and there we sat, listening to the soughing of the trees in the unaccustomed silence and shivering a little in the now deepening dusk.

The garage was closed for repairs but they housed the car and we decided to try and hitch a lift home. We were at the junction of three main

134

roads, two radiating into Suffolk and one through Norfolk. We took up our position on the Norfolk verge and waited. For the next ten minutes we watched every lorry, car and van drone up to the junction and shoot off in the other two directions. The evening grew quite dark, vehicles were switching on headlights. We began to get uneasy; no-one was obviously going to Norwich.

Then came the lights of a slow lumbering lorry rumbling and clanking like a prehistoric monster. It was the meat lorry, and Eureka! it stopped.

'You want Norwich?'

'Car broken down?'

'Yes.'

The driver grinned from a height.

'Happens to the best of us, jump in.'

He reached out a hairy dependable arm and hauled me up six feet into a roomy cabin, me in my London hat, pencil skirt and still clutching my umbrella. It was warm in the cabin and once you had negotiated round the gears surprisingly comfortable. James and I sat either side of the driver who bawled remarks at us over the noise of the engine. I could only catch these when they were directed my way and gradually took on a sense of euphoria sitting up there, high above the dark fields, experiencing for once a hundred and ninety horse power, seven gears, a shatteringly loud engine and no real resilience at all. I got the feeling that it was the road that straightened out not us. We were the juggernaut, and lesser cars with their noses to the roads were so many beetles. Even the brow of the hill was no hazard for we could see right above it. Lay-bys had a new and matey significance and so did transport cafés, where we stopped for huge thick mugs of coffee. We were knights of the road at last. I think we were slightly drunk with heights, lights and a sense of power.

In such a mood we arrived almost unexpectedly on the outskirts of Norwich. At the end of our road the driver stopped, got out and came round to open my door, his face just on a level with my feet. 'Jump,' he bawled, 'I'll catch you,' so I jumped, still slung about with umbrella and shopping bag, and landed in his arms. James, unwinding himself from the gears, followed after, with more decorum. It was only when we were firmly on the ground that we realised we'd just missed a cyclist. Did we, yes surely we did, recognise the hunch of the shoulders?

'Hitch-hiking?' cried Ladds. 'Well, well, hadn't you heard it was off-ration?'

Off guard, we asked, 'What is?'

'Petrol,' trilled Ladds cheerfully. 'It's cheaper now. I told you, some people fill their tanks with it. Try it some day.'

September

Nana is still ruler of her little kingdom in the big bedroom overlooking the garden and where her treasures are concerned she is complete mistress. No domestic help is allowed to cross the threshold and as Nana spends the mornings in bed since her hip operation the opportunity and the domestic help never synchronise anyway. Occasionally she would let me, under duress, and because the doctor was coming, bring in a vacuum cleaner and clean up, but promptly put her head under the clothes complaining that the dust got up her nose.

'Nana, it's a vacuum cleaner; it sucks *up* the dust. Much cleaner than your old Ewbank.'

'Don't believe it.'

'And even better than the dustpan and brush.'

'I know what I feel and I feel I'm sniffing up dust.'

But now she has been with us seven years or so we decided it really was time to have a mighty spring clean. We asked her if she would agree to have her room painted also. James did the asking as she is always amenable to a proposition from James as Head of the House, Nana's immediate reaction to anything being 'no', followed by a qualified acceptance, with conditions. So she slept on the proposition and decided she would submit to the room being refurbished on condition we didn't use that nasty colour we were putting in the dining-room.

'Miserable, I call it, neither one thing nor the other. Put on something cheerful and perhaps I'll have it done.'

'We thought of magnolia.'

'Magnolia? What! deep purple splodges? Couldn't stand that.'

'No, it's almost a cream with a pinky tinge.'

'All the magnolias I've seen had purple splodges, but I might consider cream. Don't know why all the modern colours are so light they show all the finger marks. Still, crean would be as cheerful as long as everyone doesn't mess it up.'

'I'll bring you a colour chart and you can choose.'

So she chose a magnolia in the end and we moved on to the tricky business of what to do with her while the painting was done, and, even more tricky, how to clear the room before the painter came.

At the first attempt Nana stood over us like a galleymaster and wouldn't let a thing be thrown away. We started with the box of mending pieces:

'Don't you take those bits of Aertex, they'll mend Roger's pants. Nor that bit of striped stuff, it matches his pyjamas. No, nor those pieces of sheeting, I'm always wanting those for patching sheets. Now what've you got? That's Aunt Jane's skunk, worth five pounds at least. Leave it alone, it'll come in useful some day...'

It'll come in useful some day, how often have I heard the phrase? I thought with a sigh of Janet's patched liberty-bodices when she came to me. Nana was the world's best make-do-and-mender and during the war was in her element, but better days were here now, and it was simply the habit that remained, not the need. We made two piles, the throw-outs and the possibles, but the first pile was still very, very small.

After lunch Nana announced she was off round the corner to draw her pension to help to pay for the paint, for she is very independent and fair to a hair's breadth, so here was our chance for a lightning swoop. Sue, Penny and I fell on to the contents of the cupboard, sorted and packed a cartonful of crockery, whipped the pictures off the walls (George Fitzwilliam by cartoonist Spy; Anxious Hearts; man on a horse crossing bridge which had been painted by her bank manager; Winston Churchill; my father; and a charming photo of Nana in her ostrich feather hat being presented with her cheque), and these we laid on top. We then dived further into the recesses of the sideboard cupboard and unearthed a bagful of fur, moths flying in clouds, a boxful of puzzles, an old dressing-gown carefully taken to pieces, and a pile of old knitting patterns, and had the lot crackling on a bonfire in no time.

By the time Nana returned the room was cleared, contents stacked and covered and she didn't miss a thing. We were able to give instructions to the painter who was to start first thing in the morning, and made arrangements for Nana to sleep in the children's room.

The first day's painting consisted of two coats on the ceiling.

At ten o'clock that night a figure in a nightgown groped its way over bare boards and between shadowy hulks of furniture draped with sheets,

137

heading firmly for the bed.

'Nana! The ceiling's still wet!'

'Doesn't matter, I shall have me head under the bed-clothes.'

'But the window's wide open because of the smell.'

'Shan't smell anything under the bedclothes. Besides smell never hurt anyone.'

'You can't put the light on you know, the curtains are all down.'

'I've undressed in Janet's room.'

'But suppose you want to get up in the night?'

'Shan't. Anyway I've got my commode. I know the way to that in the dark.'

I gave up. She slept that night among the hulks.

'I like me feather mattress,' was all she would say. 'Can't sleep on these new-fangled springs.'

It was when we reassembled the room that she began to miss things.

'Someone's taken my soap dish. I can't wash.'

'It's in the cupboard behind the newspaper wrappers.'

'Where's my box of buttons?' (Where *was* her box of buttons?)

'Someone's taken me best hat.'

'In the wardrobe.'

'Wardrobe? Whoever heard of a hat in a wardrobe? Can't reach up there. And where's the mop that I wash me feet with? I left it in me shopping bag.'

'I've put it away.'

'I don't want it put away. I want it where I can see it. Once it's away I've lost it.'

True.

By process of trial and error we sorted Nana out and put the furniture back. She decided that the carpet really needed an underfelt, but when she heard the price she changed her mind.

'Can't have that,' she said, 'we'll use brown paper, just as good. Prevents the moth too. It'll see me out.'

But after a discussion of ways and means we did persuade her to get an underfelt, through the argument, dear to her heart, that it would preserve the life of the carpet.

'And we'd better turn the carpet round too.'

'No, you don't. I've worked it all out. If you do, the worn spots at the door and the window will come at the fireplace and the sideboard. I'd sooner have 'em where they are and cover them with a mat.'

So she covered them instead and now walks on a series of mats like a chequerboard. But she has quite taken to the clean magnolia walls ('better than I expected') and is as pleased as punch.

The rash of ornaments and button boxes is creeping back again. I have no doubt that next year we shall go through the same subterfuges, each parrying the other, and will finish up with compromise, faces saved, honour satisfied, just as we have today.

✝ ✝ ✝

1958
Animals

I suppose the most popular and pleasurable addition to the animal population has been Bob, our white, shaggy-eyed, scatty, faithful mongrel. Bob thinks he's part of the family, and doesn't realise he isn't human. Certainly the children see no difference. He's just child number seven, running behind the string of youngsters, catching balls, sleeping on beds and chairs, sharing their meals, cuddling up to them. Bob, like so many other animals, just arrived on the doorstep. A woman friend of mine, Jean, came in some distress one day and said she had a small puppy which she had been hoping to keep and her mother had simply refused to have him. Mother was ninety and said she was too old to train a dog, and none of Jean's promises about training it herself had any effect. It was Mother's house and Mother's carpet and most of the day the dog would be with Mother, and the negative decision was final. At first I was very doubtful about taking him; I had suffered from too many animals, and a dog needed training and was very much *about*; you couldn't ignore a dog, just feed it once a day and muck it out once a week. But of course the whole family was in favour of Bob, Father included. They would take him to training classes, groom him, exercise him; we must have a dog. So I gave in and Jean brought him over complete with a brush, comb, worm tablets, vitamin pills, flea powder and collar. I found this rather sad; Jean needed this dog and I felt it rather cruel that at fifty odd she should not be allowed to have it. However, Bob wasn't very far away from her and she was able to pop in and see him.

As the weeks went by the training exercises petered out, partly because the class at the Church Hall was over-subscribed and partly because

139

Father was far too busy even to take him for walks and lastly and paramountly because the children hated making him do what he was told.

Nevertheless Bob was fairly amenable, didn't do much more than puppy damage, like eating the dictionary. The biggest snag was keeping him in the garden: fencing it around would cost the earth and the big gate had been taken off when Joanna grew bigger. So we had some trouble with wandering. However the neighbours gradually began to know him and the doctor round the corner said to me one day, 'Have you now got a dog? Ah, I thought so. A friendly shaggy fellow came into our garden yesterday and I thought he looked like...' - he paused for a word - 'like a Barnard kind of dog.'

‡ ‡ ‡

Each August Bank Holiday, the children trek by car or cycle to the Fête and Gymkhana at the next village. It is the chance to Show Off the Pets. One of them is almost certain to net a prize in some category. The organisers have thought up classes for everything, the best-kept animal, the best-handled animal, the most gentle-eyed, furry-tailed, obedient, appealing, natural animal, with no limit on the type of animal. There are occasionally classes for the owners too. Bob was to be entered for the mongrel class, Nicola hoping that he might cash in on the most mournful-looking or the happiest-eyed dog in the class. The fact that he had been made presentable at all was an achievement because he had earlier been painted pink by Sue and the colour wouldn't wash out.
She had painted some spots on him to vary the plainness, and in trying to remove them she succeeded in giving him an all-over apricot tint. It was attractive but wouldn't fox any judges at the gymkhana so we tried washing it out with soap and water, and that failing, detergent. He achieved some fame among the neighbours because of this apricot colouring, people thinking it was his skin showing through; besides, apricot dogs are rare.

An hour before he went, I gave him a last scrub with green soap and off he went in company with Nicola and her rabbits, and Sue who was to be his guardian.

The girls were both on bicycles and Sue had a friend behind her and Bob in her bike basket.

At half-past five the cavalcade returned with a dog-tired Bob, and two dispirited owners, having walked the bicycles five miles all told. The rabbits had won a second prize and a reserve, but Bob hadn't won anything.

'Except a box of sweets,' explained Sue lugubriously, 'and every entrant got that.' He had been entered in the mongrel class and in the 'best-handled by an under-fourteen-year-old'. Though most of the spectators agreed he was wonderfully well-handled by Sue, the hard-hearted judges didn't agree. But Bob didn't care. He just flopped down and ate and ate and then fell asleep.

I don't suppose it will stop them going to next year's gymkhana, and perhaps he'll get a prize eventually for the most rueful-looking.

November 1959

The season of charity bazaars is upon us; is there in fact ever an off-season for bazaars? To my knowledge there have followed in grim succession several Garden Fetes and Autumn Fayres, and now a Christmas Bazaar with which, for my sins, I am intimately connected. From being one-eighth of the Committee I have graduated to organising secretary. Don't ask me how it happened, it's just an insidious process and I'm landed with the end product. In a weak moment I offered to write the minutes (it seemed that I was the only one who could write) and by the next meeting I was labelled organiser.

One afternoon in the autumn we met in the church hall. The job of our committee this particular year was to take over from the previous organiser who was giving up. Mrs Wilmot was well-endowed physically and knew her own mind; she had the committee obviously well in hand and without preamble she lifted her upper half carefully on to the table and gave forth to the assembled women.

'Well, the first thing you've got to do is arrange transport. You'll want two lorries, one big one for the stall tops and a small one for the goods you're selling, which is,' fixing us with a basilisk eye, 'all the stuff I hope you've been collecting. The big lorry's the important one, it'll have to deliver at the Scout Hall the day before the Bazaar. Mind you tell the caretaker in good time, his kid's got whooping cough and that'll last from now to Christmas. Tell him the lorry'll be there at nine o'clock in the

141

morning of December 9th and will he please be there to open up. Of course,' and again I felt the long-forgotten shiver under authority's searching eye, 'of course you'll be there to supervise. Tip the lorryman five bob; might even be two men, five bob each. If you think you can do it for less you've got another think coming, 'cos you won't get 'em another year.'

I mildly asked where one got the transport.

'Where do you get the transport? Well, you write to Mr Brown of Brown's Builders, telling him you want the same lorries as last year, one open and one covered and will he be kind enough to let you have them again. Then he'll reply that he'll be pleased to do it and will you instruct Mr So-and-So in another part of the works. So you write to Mr So-and-So and if you're lucky the lorries will turn up.'

Here I intervened to say that according to the June minutes taken by my predecessor, someone had already been detailed to approach Mr Brown.

Mrs. Cantley said suddenly: 'Yes, it was Mrs Barnes.'

Mrs Barnes said, 'No, it was Mrs Cantley.'

'If you remember, dear,' said Mrs Cantley sweetly, 'the meeting was at my house, but it wasn't my job to do it.'

The red light of battle flared up in Mrs Barnes's eye. Foreseeing hostilities I hurriedly referred back to the minutes but unfortunately they read that Mr Brown was to be approached, without naming the approacher, so I made a mental note that in future I'd better name the person proposed for the job.

'Then,' said Mrs Wilmot, 'there's Mr Braithwaite who'll set up the stall tops. Ten bob I give him and probably his pal too.'

'Billy Braithwaite's poorly,' said someone, 'something the matter with his stomach. And hasn't he retired?'

'Course he's retired, so's his pal. How on earth else do you think he'd find the time. But you'll have to notify him.'

'I don't reckon Billy ought to be asked this year,' said worried Mrs Davy; 'he's got a duodenal ulcer.'

'That's his brother,' retorted Wilmot, 'that's Abey. Billy's the cross-eyed one who married Lily Riches. She died on him winter before last, chronic bronchitis. He's like a dog without a master. Still, he's got plenty of time on his hands.'

'That's right,' beamed Mrs Davy, relieved at having got it straight at

142

last. 'Abey had the ulcer and the seven children. I remember...'

'Are we having a meeting or aren't we?' thundered Wilmot. 'Madam Secretary, put down Billy Braithwaite for stall tops. Ten shilling tip and same for pal, and somebody'd better be there early when the lorry arrives.'

I made a note.

'Then,' continued Mrs Wilmot relentlessly, 'there's those big posters. The caretaker likes 'em ten days beforehand to put up outside. And take down some of my special paste to stick 'em with; it sticks better than other people's. Don't use drawing pins outside; they rust in the bad weather. Anyway Alfie Jenkins'll see to all that for you - he runs a newsagent's and sundries - and he'll bring the paste. Now where you *will* want drawing pins is on the stalls, to pin down all that crepe paper they twiddle up the sides. Alfie'll bring those too; don't let the stallholders bring their own pins, the tops fall off. But,' as an afterthought, 'they'll have to bring their own sheets.'

I wondered if they were all staying the night, which wouldn't have surprised me, but no, these sheets were to cover the trestles.

'Teas!' said Mrs Wilmot rising again to the attack. 'There's that thing in the kitchen, gas ring, I think it is...'

'Boiler,' murmured Mrs Cantley.

'Gas ring,' ripped Mrs Wilmot without taking breath. 'You'll write to Mr Tring of the Gas Board asking for whatever it was last year, and you'll get no reply so you'll write again asking them to attend to it and after a few days you'll get a letter saying yes and they'll put it in. Whatever it is...'

'Boiler,' said Mrs Cantley.

'Gas ring! Besides all that,' here Wilmot wagged a finger, 'there's the helpers' badges. Mrs Maggs makes those.'

'Are they actually badges?' asked someone rashly. 'Weren't they rosettes last year?'

'Rosettes!' The word was mud. 'Maggs isn't going to bother with rosettes. Too much gathering.'

'Couldn't she use the gathering foot on the machine?'

'No, she can't. If you want rosettes you can make 'em yourself. Maggs makes little square red badges, with 'Committee' written on for the Committee members, so see the right people get 'em. Now there's this business of cakes, and here you need eyes in the back of your head. Cakes for the cake stall get taken to refreshments if you don't watch and then there's hell on. Two years ago there was a fine fuss - especially as Cakes's eldest girl, Jessie Markley, the tall one with the lisp, had just jilted Refreshments' middle boy, Tom. So there was a rare rumpus and we don't want another. The upshot of that was that we lost Mrs Markley to the Bran Tub, which was a waste.' She looked nostalgic. 'Markley was a dab hand with a sponge cake,' said she. I duly noted the point.

And so we progressed to the burning question of the afternoon which was who was to take on the Grocery stall. Mrs Philpott had done it last year, but she was expecting again and felt she could not cope in the small amount of space between the stall and the back wall. 'It isn't that I'm not willing,' she wrote, 'but when I turn round for change I knock over all the Vim tins and cornflake packets. So please excuse this year and oblige, Annie Philpott.'

So we tried to oblige Mrs Philpott by finding someone else, but, as we who have had experience know, it was like looking for a needle in a haystack.

I should think Groceries should be easy enough,' Mrs Wilmot. 'Everyone has groceries in the house: a tin of beans, a pot of jam, a dishmop...'

'Jam is Pickles and Preserves,' piped up Mrs Barnes.

'Dishmop's Hardware,' tendered little Mrs Davy.

'Heavens above, this place is like a trade union,' exploded Mrs Wilmot. 'What about you, Mrs Cantley? You haven't got a stall this year'.

'I couldn't possibly, Madam Chairman. My husband likes me home at nights and my daughter's expecting...the amount of knitting I have to do for her is colossal.'

'Right, we'll put you down for a matinee coat for Fancy Goods. Mrs Barnes, what about you?'

But Mrs Barnes had a heart, and it seemed Mrs Noble had the Choral Society, and Mrs Jenkins her Dogs. Even Mrs Wilmot's bullying couldn't make them budge. So in the end the matter was delegated to little Mrs Davy to try and find a substitute. I felt sorry for Mrs Davy. It seemed to me that the weakest went to the wall.

As we passed on to the questions of the Opener and the Bouquet the afternoon grew dusky and the tinkle of teacups began to be heard in the kitchen. Gratefully we abandoned the Cold War and fell on our cups of tea.

On returning home I looked at my notes. Apart from Billy Braithwaite

and Pal, ten bob, I seemed to have several garbled phrases:
  Watch out tops fall off;
  Boiler/gas ring, avoid explosion at all costs;
  Maggs won't gather;
  Cakes to the Cake;
and one particularly cryptic one which could have applied equally to paper, sheets or people -
  Pin them down next time.

December 1959
  Nicola and I peer into the murky depths of the tank of the washing-machine and proceed to tie a sheet tightly above its open top to make a roof, so that it looks for all the world like a boiled pudding. Why are we doing this? You might well guess. I have been landed with the Cosmetic Stall at the Christmas Bazaar and we are manufacturing products for the same. Down in the depths of the tank are several pounds of washing soda, scented but slightly soggy, and we are trying to turn them into bath salts. It was an experiment. We had mixed up a little eggcupful of liquid, composed of lavender water, cochineal and water and shaken it up with the soda in a preserving jar. But the resultant mess was too wet. It was obvious that the only necessary additions to the soda were scent and colouring so we were now trying to get rid of the water. Putting the concoction in the oven had caused the grains to melt and stick together; putting it in the sunroom was too slow. So here we were trying to spin it dry. Because the top of the washing tank was open to the air and the crystals would fly out, we were making a roof, like a tent.
  'Do other folk ever do things like this?' enquired Nic, pulling the sheet tight.
  'No, never, I'm sure,' I muttered, fastening the tent with a safety-pin. 'But then perhaps we're ingenious. We'd be good on a desert island. Anyway we can't waste two pounds of washing soda already scented. And it's Sunday so we can't get any more if we wanted.' I wondered if it was the judgment of a higher court than ours for manufacturing on Sunday, but dammit it was for charity. It crossed my mind, not for the first time, that we do some puerile things for bazaars hoping that the gullible public will pay for them in a spirit of unselfishness when they wouldn't dream of doing so in a shop.
  Right from the moment that we sent out the appeal notices for the

145

Christmas Bazaar written in the children's spidery and Nana's vigorous handwriting, the house has been in a turmoil. First came the trickle of gifts: soaps, deodorants, hair oil and money; then the visit to the wholesalers, wandering between dim shelves of boxes which spilled out colourful contents when ripped open by the assistant. Then came the weighing-up of one product against another from the selling point of view, shampoo against toothpaste, aspirin versus sticking-plaster, brilliantine against hair-conditioner or after-shave against both. What innocents we were in a cut-throat world, and how daring we felt when we bought £10 worth of stuff knowing we only had six pounds in hand; and what a shock finding out on the subsequent invoice that 25% and 50% purchase tax had pushed the total to eleven pounds eight shillings.

And later came a pleasant surprise in the form of a quarter gross of gift boxes, mixed soap, talc and perfume from a neighbour, and a man at that, who brought them round one night with all the excitement of a conjurer bringing objects out of a hat. Then the niggling job of assembling odd items of soap, shampoo and salts into respectable cellophaned packages. Later, in a losing struggle with cardboard squares and plastic lids I passed the whole lot on to Percy, my versatile eighty-year-old pal, who assembled them for me in what seemed to be no time at all. Oh the hopeful, idiotic, time-consuming misery of the English charity bazaar, entrenched in the tradition, woven into the fabric of the English character! Women's character, that is. You'll never find a man engaged in this process of attrition; he'll buy five hundred articles wholesale and flog the lot, gain or loss, and if it's a loss he'll pay up with a grin and disappear next year. Or if he's a gambler he'll buy a thousand matchboxes, six of which have a special coupon inside and if you get a coupon you win a prize: simple as that.

I suppose it's a mixture of vanity and pride that makes women work so hard at the job; vanity because they think that what they are producing will be irresistible to the customers (I'm always sure of that and so is Nana), and pride in the craftsmanship of it. Undaunted, we push on.

December 20th - The Bazaar

Of the day itself I am still too exhausted to write in detail, but we decorated the stall with red and white swags and twiddly paper. It is extraordinary how no-one, even I, seems to be able to cover a stall-top of two-by-two-inch laths with anything but spiralling crêpe paper, but when we had finished titivating it with tinsel and filling it with the many-coloured packages it looked really lovely, red, white and sparkling. We prepared and manned the stall from twelve noon till eight in the evening. In the beginning a phalanx of stony-faced housewives from the town stood there solidly waiting for us to reduce everything and even offered us cut prices. At this, my helper, a staunch old campaigner, got the battle light in her eyes. 'Not on your Nelly,' said she. Then to make matters worse a fellow stallholder spoke her mind about us charging less than market prices. It was my turn to get the battle light. I had collected, made or bought wholesale, most of the stuff on the stall and was going to sell it as I jolly well pleased. However as the afternoon wore on sales and tempers improved and by teatime we were left with a hardcore of toothpaste and shampoo and felt we could relax and go and seek Refreshments.

'How are you doing?' asked little Mrs Davy confidentially over the tea and sausage rolls.

'Surviving. All the glamorous stuff has gone but there's enough soap and denture cream left to supply an old folks' home.'

'Never mind, dear, one good push and you're finished.'

'I'm finished already,' said I, reaching for another cup.

But my star was in the ascendant. When I came back I found I'd had an unexpected Fairy Godmother; Mrs Wilmot the inflexible, Mrs Wilmot of the basilisk eye, had bought the remaining lot. We had made thirty-two pounds fifteen. I suppose you could say it was worth nine months' sweat and planning.

But I do wonder!

August 1960

There is now a new dimension to Eaton End; every July we have what is fast becoming a continental invasion. In reality only one bewildered teenager at a time arrives at our place from over the Channel, but like a magnet he or she attracts every foreigner in the district. It all began with the twinning of Norwich and Rouen. Representatives of the Norwich municipality, including James, splendid in his Treasurer's cocked hat and fur-edged gown, went over to Rouen to set off the twinning and very soon afterwards Marie-Claire Renouard, daughter of one of Rouen's officials, came over to Norwich. The idea of a continental exchange has spread like a forest fire since the war. Round about July strange faces appear among the normal Norfolk dumplings, and youngsters of various nationalities are to be seen holding shopping bags for middle-aged English mums, or roaming in loose groups looking for discos, or eating hamburgers at the snack bars. The reason for their aimless wanderings is that the English children are still at school during most of July, so the various hostesses have to amuse their guests themselves and the telephones run hot with frantic phonings to other mothers to help out. It's no surprise that our well-worn tennis court becomes dotted with polyglot teenagers all trying to understand each other in broken English. Then, at the end of July, their English counterparts are able to link up with them and flood down to the sea or to the swimming pool or into the country, and the parents breathe again.

But not for long. Promptly, as July finishes, the continentals go back for their statutory holiday by their own seaside and in September our youngsters join them for the return visit. And so it goes on. Nicola of course is our present exchanger.

Last summer Marie-Claire was here for a month. It was just such a summer as the one when Joanna was born, with long days of light and shade, of sunlight through flowers and of fanlike branches lit to a green transparency against the dark hearts of the trees. Several times we were on the edge of drought, but never quite there. I remember lying on the grass and watching the patterns of the branches, a rare thing for me to do, but with Marie-Claire life was restful. I worried sometimes how to amuse her, but she was on the whole very self-sufficient. For one thing she did not eat breakfast and so appeared downstairs at about ten or eleven o'clock, which suited me very well. She liked to sunbathe or just sit in the garden, for in Rouen they have only a roof garden, and one of my memories of that extraordinary summer is of Marie-Claire in a turquoise swimsuit stretched out in a deckchair, the sun running round the edge of her like gold thread. I painted a portrait of her in a pink gingham dress and Lynette's son took her sailing and somehow the three weeks before our schools broke up were whittled away. I had worried, too, about the food, for normally we didn't feed nine in Cordon Bleu style, but Marie-

Claire, on a postcard propped on the telephone for posting, found us quite 'sympathique', and the food 'not bad at all'. I know she liked the strawberry jam and the home-made salad cream because she took the recipes back with her.

In the last week of her visit she put to us a rather tentative question: 'Madame, am I to save my fare back to London or may I spend the money to have my hair bleached? Mama allows me to do this.'

Bleached hair? M'm-m. Well, I suppose, if Mama says so...

We had not really considered the journey back, so we made enquiries and found that the boat-train left Victoria at 9.30 a.m. and there was certainly no train from Norwich that would catch that. James and I decided we could go up by car and take the family, then we could have a day out and Marie-Claire could afford to bleach her hair. It meant starting at five o'clock in the morning, with a packed lunch and everyone squashed in the back, but we did it, hoping eventually to finish up at the Zoo in Regent's Park. There were of course snags, there always are. We had a puncture halfway there, but we did get Marie-Claire to Victoria in time and I realised as we waved goodbye that she had really loved England and didn't want to go.

Turning our nose from Victoria, we made tracks for the Zoo, first visit ever for the children, and we gave ourselves up to the fun of it.

How do you assess a child's first view of a zoo? Much hilarity judging from their shrieks. Sheer wonder at the penguins and elephants; shivers in the snake-house where the wretched reptiles coiled and teetered, and flickered at us through the glass. Mute unbelief in the giraffe enclosure where the creatures swanned around in dignified hauteur. Everything enchanted them: the shapes of giraffes and camels; incredible textures like the pelts of polar bears and porcupines, and extraordinary ways of getting about like the monkeys with their convoluted jumps, screeching like rusty ratchets at us all. A lovely morning.

It was only when we started to picnic on the grass that we realised that Marie-Claire had sat on the pineapple trifle and squashed it, so we tucked in, instead, to a kind of pineapple mousse. I thought wryly that the Italians call trifle 'English soup' and that's just about what it was.

When we arrived home, a hundred miles away, we found Nic had left her best coat outside the giraffe house. Could it have been their lofty superiority that drove such mundane things right out of her head? Whatever it was, it was damned annoying; the coat was new and of a pretty shade of blue, bought at a sale and would take twice as much to replace.

However we had quite a eulogistic letter from Marie-Claire some weeks afterwards, well-chewed by Bob the dog as it lay on the mat, and frantically put together by us in case it suggested boat times for Nicola, whose return visit was due. Nic had been accepted for a pre-university year at a crammer's in Cambridge and needed the French for furbishing up her A-levels. Bob meanwhile considers himself one of the family and even joins in evening prayers.

Not all the foreigners were as adaptable as Marie-Claire, nor could they speak English as freely. There seemed to be two ways of coping with this impasse, either to speak very slowly and clearly in a kind of pidgin English or merely to talk in French, which to me seemed cheating. The family is very rude about my pidgin English. They say it sounds ridiculous and that I am apt to forget and try it out on them! I get a withering look from Roger and the tart retort, 'Remember me? I'm English.'

James and Nana had their own ways of dealing with the problem: James shouts cheerfully, and Nana enunciates very slowly as to a retarded child. Chacun à son goût.

It is not only the language that causes tensions; it is the responsibility of feeding and entertaining these would-be linguists. Yves also propped up a card to post, which was not quite as complimentary as Marie-Claire's: 'The people are kind but the food is bad.'

A body blow, just what I had feared: feed the foreigner and you have to feed the family. So we improved the food and that week my household bills went up by a third. ('More fool you,' said James somewhat unsympathetically.) Moreover Yves was inclined to sit chattering

French with his brother from a billet down the road. Why do foreign conversations always sound like quarrelling? In French they sound like argumentative starlings, and in Flemish like a throat-clearing competition. What a waste the whole complicated arrangement is when the youngsters sit there jabbering in their own tongue!

But they seemed to need human companionship as much as the language. The only really strong-minded customer was Jean-Paul nearby, who would not speak French under any circumstances. 'I do not know how to spik it,' said he with a grin.

But worse than food or language are the arrangements made without our knowledge on our very phone in opposition to our carefully sweated-out programme. Ghislaine, a Belgian, on a day planned for the sea, invited a whole tennis party from a village seven miles away where her German boyfriend was billeted. By the time we found out it was too late to notify everyone concerned so we upped with the family as planned and left Ghislaine behind to cope. Apparently a cosmopolitan crowd arrived in our absence with racquets and sandwiches, much to the demoralisation of Nana, now eighty-four and no admirer of the Entente Cordiale.

I could go on with fervour about the perplexing ways of our overseas guests but to them this behaviour of course is perfectly logical. If our habits were identical they wouldn't be here. The freedom of England obviously goes to the youngsters' heads, habits such as dropping in on people, going for cycle rides, being allowed to wander round the city unaccompanied (ours is a small and innocuous city), the general informality of our conversation, customs and letters. We were mollified to find that they liked our ice-cream, fish and chips, and domestic animals, and on the whole found it did not rain as much as they thought.

In return for a somewhat harassing month's holiday (for us) Yves sent a charming thank-you letter, finishing up with, 'Please give from me a bisquit at Bob,' which warmed my heart but made me despair of his month's tuition. Due to all that French chattering in the sunroom, no doubt.

Desperate Ditty

Will you bring your charming French boy here to tea, Mrs. C.?
It might improve his English, eating cake with you and me.
I really must confess it will help me thro' a mess
If you then could ask *my* French boy for a spree, Mrs. C.

The problem is that in July our children are not free
So entertaining Jean and Paul will fall to you and me.
I can't speak French for toffee and I make most awful coffee
Will you bring your French boy therefore here to tea, Mrs. C.?

Paul's carried shopping-baskets till his fingers are aflame.
And Jacques, Pierre and Marie-Claire are doing just the same.
I've played a tennis single till my bicep muscles tingle
And seen the sights a bicyclette more times than I can name.

I'll have your Jean for tennis if you'll take Paul to the sea,
Then Mrs. X is party-throwing for her Anne-Marie,
With French and English twinning, it's hard to know who's winning
But the only mug who's learning French is poor old frantic me.

October '60

In the early autumn Nic returned from France.
We met her off the boat-train, a slim sophisticated
figure with the latest T.B. look (lank hair, huge eyes,
white lipstick). She was slung about with a bottle
of Côte-du-Rhône and some French records under
one arm, while two terrapins and a packet of worms
squirmed in a jar under the other. Both hands
were occupied with suitcases. In answer to our
query as to How she Got On, she breathed
ecstatically (she could just breathe), 'C'était
formidable,' in the smoothest French accent
and added, 'Well four sons and a boat on
the Seine!' What do you expect!'
We relieved her of everything but the
livestock from which she refused to be parted.
'How did you get them through the customs?'
'Oh, I managed.'
'What are you going to do with them if you are off to Cambridge?'
'Take them with me. I simply must have a pet in Cambridge, I simply
must, and they won't let you have rabbits.'
'How big do terrapins grow?'
'Oh, they don't.'

These were lively little fellows, like tortoises with tails. We put them in a fairly deep baking-tin on the solid top of our outside water tank. The second day one climbed over the edge of the baking-tin and disappeared and we all thought it had fallen and drowned through a small opening in the tank. (Do they drown? Where's the encyclopaedia?) We peered, with one eye shut, down the shafts of sunlight that illumined the bottom of the tank but only saw tins, chocolate papers and rubbish. No terrapin. Even Bob, snuffling around, failed to find it. But it turned up, thoroughly withdrawn, some hours later, having toppled three feet on to the concrete. Replaced, it started a persistent climb up the side of the tin again.

The next day they both disappeared and no amount of squinting down the water tank would reveal them. All we are left with is a jar of small red worms which squirm about until they too gradually topple out of the jar.

‡   ‡   ‡

James and I went over to Cambridge this week to see Nic in her new habitat and to combine it with a lecture James was giving at the Arts Theatre. My overwhelming impression of Cambridge that afternoon was of cold and cheerlessness, so different from the warm airs that cosseted us in June, when ambling along the riverside beneath the willows. But then this was one of the bitterest days of the autumn and Cambridge is very flat and vulnerable to winds. The sitting room at Grange House where James dropped me was fireless and I had to wait half an hour for Nicola to finish a lecture at a tutor's house some way from the school.

After my spending the half-hour with a six-month-old *Illustrated London News*, Nicola blew in, flat-heeled and tousled from having cycled across the fields. She changed into high-heeled shoes and put up her hair in a French pleat, and we went out for a meal. 'I know just the place,' she said, 'for something a little bit different. How about some continental cuisine?' So we fought through the bitter cold to a restaurant called 'The Gardenia', Greek-run, where we had Côtelette Milanaise and Greek lokma, and were eyed steadily by the Greek waiter from start to finish. There seemed to be a kind of yearning about him that made me look anew at Nicola. We'd always taken her so much for granted as simply the eldest daughter that I realised now that she was an attractive girl with lovely colouring, and with something perhaps indefinable added to it. He couldn't have been looking at her mature mum in a red fox hat, though that seemed to intrigue him too. I got the impression that he would devour us hungrily, lokma and all, once he was off the leash.

With this at the back of my mind we went to the Arts Theatre to pick up James and deposited Nicola back in her icy nest about ten o'clock into the tender care of a young lady warden in a shortie housecoat and sandals. Was she a nun too? I felt that, for a Convent cramming school, Nic was in liberal hands.

But there is something special about Cambridge. When Nicola and I were sheltering in a telephone booth from the Fen winds, the gusty streets outside full of undergrads on bicycles, their gowns flapping crow-like in the blast, we found 'Téléphonez-moi chérie' written in biro behind the glass frame and below it, 'Je vous aime.' It wouldn't have happened, I thought, in Norwich.

November 9th '60

This year in addition to the usual firework celebrations we survived a Hallowe'en party for ten under-fourteens, schoolfriends of Sue. It was arranged entirely by Sue without any help from me, except for five shillings that she asked me for towards the end. She organised it with the help of the younger three girls; in fact I think we might dub them The Quartette now as they have an almost corporate existence of their own. Roger at sixteen hardly belongs to us but to some half-world of his own, peopled by school, girl friend, youth club, the Sir Thomas Browne Society and his shadow henchman, Dick Crayshaw from over the fence. His time is spent, when not at school, in the attic or hammering in the shed, or making innumerable journeys on his bike to town, or at other people's firesides.

The Quartette saved up their money and allocated it between buns, bananas, orangeade, candles and prizes. The garage was turned into a barn for the occasion with much borrowing from the house of odd pieces of lino to cover puddles of motor oil, kitchen chairs, old tables and hurricane lamps. I felt rather sorry for the guests, little girls in good dresses who had to be soused while bobbing apples and sit on hard chairs in a draughty garage. But it was highly successful they told me, except for the fact that Roger and Dick had let off bangers among the girls' nyloned ankles, and the more adventurous guests had rushed out into the dark garden, where in the pale mists of Hallowe'en among wet leaves and the decaying detritus of summer they had played murder, screaming to their hearts' content. Sue did not consider this a snag, but I did.

At about nine o'clock, the ten satisfied, slightly dishevelled sub-teeners said their thanks and were whisked off home in the fog.

‡   ‡   ‡

September 1961

Nicola is not the only one who has been abroad; a year later we've had quite an epidemic of it. Roger has been to Spain, Janet to Switzerland with the school and Sue to Rouen: all in the cheapest possible way, camping, exchanges, school trips. Now in September they are all safely gathered in and I have as mementoes a pile of brightly-coloured postcards dotted with snowy peaks, cathedrals, and flamencos, each describing new and heady experiences, mainly food and boys, which is the stage we seem to have reached. Roger, en route for Spain, stops off in London to spend a day with Geoff, home from Singapore for a spell before going off to Ghana. So there plops on the mat a card of Buckingham Palace:

> 'Dear Mum. Hope you are surviving. Uncle took us out to
> the Tower of London then out to dinner. We had pork chops,
> roast taters and beans.'

Why do my children always write about food? Do I starve them? It reminded me of an earlier one from Roger, 'Went out to tea and ate twenty-one pickled onions.' Probably his hostess counted them in amazement.

From Paris we were informed that he had ' seen the I fell Tower and drink in France is very expensive and I can't understand what the French are saying'. Spain produced only a brief note to say the mosquitoes were enormous, 'zooming at you like jet planes and the blooming grasshoppers are four inches long'. Roger is always to the point.

The next batch came from Janet in Switzerland, a precise diary, food orientated. On the boat train from England she noted:

> 'We had gorgeous breakfast, corn flakes, 4 rashers bacon, 1
> sausage, 1 tomato, 2 toast, 2 coffee, all to myself. 1 girl got left
> behind.
> P.S. The girl has been found.'

155

But, alas! the blow-out had repercussions.

'Arrived Paris 6.15 p.m. and dined at a cafe. The food we eat there I was sick from it. Went in coach round Paris and I wrote postcards for three hours.

P.P.S. We sightseed Paris, a place full of lights.'

From Switzerland the débâcle continued.

'Arrived Martigny and caught the train up the mountain for Les Marecottes. Breakfast and dinner I did not have because I had been sick six times.'

But after that events improved, and details of one Alphonse, a chef, thereafter took the place of food and scenery.

On the 29th there was actual mention of the St Bernard Pass and snowballs, plus a small description of the overhead railway at Chamonix, where they missed, by half an hour, being plunged into the valley.

Lastly, on the 30th August, Alphonse 'buried the cheese and the hotel staff were angry'. We were intrigued about this one; why did he bury the cheese? Was it too maggoty? Or was he hiding his culinary efforts?

However, the bright bubble of excitement was eventually pricked; on the 30th also they packed and left, Alphonse accompanying them to the end of the mountain railway.

We asked Janet on return about the buried cheese, but it turned out to be a mis-spelling for 'burned'. Well, it had us all intrigued. And the diary was a cheering change from the usual British moans about drains in Venice.

That just left Sue in Rouen. She had been warned by Nicola, now Big Experienced Sister, to scrub her neck while abroad, the French being pernickety people. But Sue, in a card of St Ouen Cathedral at sunset, retaliated smartly. 'You needn't worry about washing. They don't here. Love to Bob. Sue.'

A few days later a second latter sent us all into deep gloom.

'It's only half-past ten and I have the whole day in front of me and nothing to do. I'm so BORED. They won't let me out without a chaperone and everyone's too busy to care and I wish I were home again.'

Well there was nothing we could do but write, and by the time we did that Marie-Claire's large family had arrived back in Rouen from holiday and Sue had had permission to contact them.

I shouldn't like to give the impression that the whole exchange business was unrelieved gloom. Seen in retrospect we have had fun out of it, still do, have made some good friends and hope to experience some French hospitality ourselves one day. All it needs for success is a bit of tolerance, and, let's face it, endless ingenuity.

But sometimes I do fear for the Entente Cordiale.

† † †

October '61

A voice comes out of the twilight this autumnal afternoon as I near the house and a hunched-up figure dawdles into view. Penny with a satchel on her shoulder and a carefully held box.

'My cake didn't come out right...'

'Oh?'

'I dropped it just before I put it in the oven.'

'Oh!'

'Then I dropped it after it came out. That didn't improve matters. It's rather flat.'

'Oh dear!'

'I expect Roger'll eat it.'

She comes in from shopping in the city.

'Shut your eyes, I've got something for you.'

Slam! Two whisky tot glasses.

'And something eatable but I've had some of them because they were rather bashed.'

Slam! One pound of eating apples (minus one or two).

'Here's a nice red one, Mummy, eat that now.'

So I eat it now.

Phone-talk:

'Oh George is nice. He's got fine drawn skin as if there wasn't enough to go round and blue eyes and is very tall and has a mind like a butterfly.'

'Harvey is a dish. He's got a super sexy figure, tight jeans, low slung belt and a gorgeous open shirt.'

So that's what they like in this year of grace 1961.

Easter, 1962

Is it any wonder one's daughters are not practical around the house when the learning that occupies their days has no relation to practicality. It is vacation time again and I peer over Nicola's shoulder as she sits hunched up over her papers. She is wrestling with the answers to the following:

Discuss the range of Milton's experiments with seventeenth century poetic forms.
Examine some of the metaphysical elements in Herbert's poetry.
Write an essay on Chaucer's use of innuendo, or the relationship one observes between the new scientific philosophy embodied in Bacon's work and the literary tradition that developed towards the end of the seventeenth century.

And so on.

I could substitute a few questions myself that have never yet been set by an examiner, for instance:

How do you write an obituary letter?
Can you explain that there is only limited hot water in the house in a. French   b. Flemish   c. German
What is the secret of preventing a soufflé collapsing before a supper party (or even an overweight guest collapsing after a supper party)?
Define the precise difference between osteochondro-dystrophy and multiple epiphyseal dysplasia, or sinusitis and sinovitis, come to that.
What chemicals remove the following stains:
     creosote
     biro scribble on walls
     cod liver oil on carpets
     gentian violet anywhere?
How and where do you apply for an employment card?
Describe the first and second stages of childbirth. (On second thoughts better not try to do anything of the kind.)

I suppose they will learn about these things sooner or later; in the University of the Home probably. But they won't get any degrees for it, except perhaps a Diploma for Survival.

I am now mulling over another question to add to the previous ones. How do you diplomatically get rid of Boy Friends one and two in time for the arrival of number three? It can't be a new problem; mothers must have coped with it for generations.

Tonight Nicola goes to bed early because she is shooting coypus with Jeremy and William at five-thirty tomorrow morning. On the marshes somewhere. Boy friend three, Charles from Cambridge, arrives off the boat-train from Germany at nine-thirty and is heading straight for here. Just as she is nicely in the bath after tea, Jeremy rings up to remind her about the coypus.

'Haven't forgotten, dying to come,' she breathes over the phone, clad in a towel. 'And of course you'll come to breakfast afterwards. No, don't be evasive, it's no trouble at all, Mum'll love to have you. Oh, you want to plan the rest of the morning? From about when?' The voice became guarded. 'Well I'm not sure about *after* breakfast, I really have another engagement. Anyway we can discuss it later. See you...'

I hiss that we have no milk and won't get any before 8.30 a.m. and go on to find out we have little butter and less marmalade as tomorrow is our stocking-up day. So Father, arriving home for tea in a rosy glow from a successful meeting, is turned round at the door to fetch six cartons of milk from the machine.

I do some rapid calculations. At eight a.m. tomorrow we feed the family, at nine Nicola, Jeremy and William, and at ten, Charles. I reckon the food would be a bit thin for the last four, so for the first time in my life I borrow butter from next door. I breathe a pious hope that Nic despatches Boy Friends one and two before three arrives. Or doesn't it matter?

Later

She hardly did, and it didn't matter. Jeremy and William were wrenched from drinking coffee to rush her down to the station to meet Charles. Nicola had obviously confessed she had him in tow, and the three came back together quite cheerfully for more coffee at ten. But I noticed Jeremy and friend then discreetly withdrew, leaving the field to Charles. Ah well, I suppose this is only a beginning.

159

May 1962

We have this year managed to take the whole family to France, down to Nice, in a big old Austin liable to break down at least once on a long journey and actually doing so five times. Roger was co-driver, having passed his test one month beforehand, and he drove well except for a near-miss with a bus in the main square of Rouen. By less than a metre and with only a single scream each from Marie-Claire and her mother (whom we had picked up as our guides for the day), we slid past it.

The general set-up of the holiday seemed promising. We were going to stay in a villa which in its time had been a small monastery, Domaine du Christ. It had been left to a Norwich man, a Mr Carpenter, by a Free French pilot who unfortunately was shot down before the end of the war, but Carpenter was quite unable to take possession due to the French system of inheritance tax which he could not pay, and he therefore let it out for some years to a farmer and his wife, who acted as caretakers and grew carnations and vines on the stepped terraces around it. Eventually Carpenter moved in, and to make a living let the house out to English families as a summer villa. It was as a rented villa that we originally took it, the price being incredibly low.

Before we actually clinched the matter, Carpenter had decided to turn it into a guesthouse and we were its first guests ('Guinea-pigs,' said Roger). We found that he had taken on a young helper, Jon Chapple, who had helped him convert it, structurally, from a tumbledown villa to an elegant hostelry. Carpenter ate with us and acted as mine host, reading his plays and poems to us after meals of carnation-fed rabbit stuffed with herbs, accompanied by the usual salade Nicoise. James as always relaxed and gave himself up to these impromptu evenings but the youngsters were restive, especially Roger and Nic, and preferred to go down to Nice in Jon Chapple's car.

After three evening meals of rabbit and Nice salad we began to suspect that Carpenter couldn't afford to feed us. James had paid a deposit some months before, but had refused to pay the first week's board also in advance until he had some idea of the set-up. I now decided that he'd better do this or we'd be eating rabbit Niçoise till the end of the holiday, so he talked with Carpenter, paid up and immediately the menu improved. We then felt relaxed enough to go into the huge kitchen and watch Madame Cabri, the farmer's wife, conjuring up little miracles of Provençal fare. Carpenter himself had never quite mastered the language and spoke a music-hall hybrid of French and English. He and James would amble round the estate peering at the vines and the vegetables, flipping over a leaf here and pruning a branch there.

'They're poussing well this year,' says Carpenter, 'poussing very well. Regardez these healthy shoots. Formidable, considering they've been attacked en suite by the mistral and the gel, and now the bête.'

He is building with Jon's help a Provencal fireplace and needs some extra stone. So off they go, he and James, to the stonemason's where he rummages among piles of masonry, muttering abstractedly to the patient Niçois in charge of it.

'I want,' he says, 'une pierre like this,' he measures with his hands, 'pour une fireplace.' The stonemason nods.

'Can you ménager une piece this size,' queries Carpenter, 'say 30 centimetres by 40?'

'Oui, oui.' The Niçois searches in the corner of the yard.

'Puis-j'avoir un red piece?' asks Carpenter plaintively. 'Je n'aime pas the green. Is that alright?'

'Bien sur, M'sieur.' There is a kind of telepathy between them as there is with children.

The village, Roman de Bellet, had its own wine which we saw growing on the terrace and a mountainous hinterland behind, which stretched to the perfume town of Grasse and St Paul de Vence and to the intimidating Wolf Gorge. Dramatic country, rugged and awesome. But for Nice itself we didn't much care. It was a moneyed place and the beach was parcelled out in private plots. The only free area was by the harbour, where we had to undress on the rocks and here my three blossoming daughters were scrutinised by the French voyeurs gathered in the shallows below. So objectionable was this that we moved over to Villefranche, near the promontory where Somerset Maugham had a villa, but finding that on the peninsula too the beaches were fenced off, we snuggled down in thoroughly Bolshie mood at Villefranche itself.

One rewarding result of lying around and eating out was that we absorbed at first hand how the French lived.

One day we were picnicking, English fashion, on the hot stony beach, our wine bottle drifting at the water's edge, our banana skins and ourselves fast deteriorating in the Midi sun, when over the slope behind filed a French family, Mama, Papa, Grandmère and Francois. Smartly they trotted to the edge of the sea and unpacked a chaise-longue, a folding table and four chairs, and all the impedimenta necessary for eating: napkins, plates and cutlery, vinegar and oil, wine and glasses. Grandmère whipped out her knitting, M'sieur his little sunhat and his Paris-Matin and started to read.

While we gazed, fascinated, at all this efficiency, Madame discreetly manoeuvred herself out of a sheath dress and revealed herself in a backless swimsuit. She whisked a garment off Francois and he too was ready for the sea. Madame's performance in the water was as brisk as her undressing, two minutes flat, and after that ten minutes on the sunbed, well clear of the stones which were torturing the rest of us.

At this juncture, James, a lobster-pink Englishman if ever there was one, who burns if he exposes a toe, emerged to marvel at it all from under his parasol. But Madame was not aware of onlookers; she got up, zipped herself into her dress with great sangfroid and attacked the hamper. Chicken legs, lettuce hearts, French roll, apples, grapes and the inevitable wine followed each other on to the table. The family tucked in their napkins and ate, bolt upright, in sacred silence like a ritual, with fixed stares over the sea.

I must confess that at this point the midday haze and the effects of our own meal overcame us and we fell asleep. When we came to, the hamper had been closed, the furniture collapsed and the family had vanished over the curve. The whole shimmering noonday beach was ours again.

'Phew!' said I. That's the way to do it. Efficiency. Organisation. French flair.'

162

'Nonsense!' countered James phlegmatically. 'Most unrelaxing. They'll all have ulcers in ten years' time. Meals on holiday should be eaten semi-recumbent as the Romans did. Personally I'm not bringing collapsible furniture nearly a thousand miles, in addition to six people and their luggage. Nature's provided nice flat stones, let's sit on them,' and he wriggled himself into a hole among the wreckage and disappeared beneath the parasol.

I wished, as I collected tins and peel and rammed them into a polythene bag, that Nature had, as well as stones, supplied us each with an air cushion. But perhaps the French have that advantage too.

On the way back we stayed a night in Rouen with the Renouards feeling that we had at last met up with people who were really old friends in spirit. I must have known as much about their idiosyncrasies as they about mine. ('Madame Renouard, she not like to wash up,' Yves had once said. 'Tell her,' said I, 'that Madame Barnard not like to wash up either.') We really felt that evening, through a haze of cigar smoke, and after a superb dinner, that we really could explain one country to the other.

'Is it really true,' asked Madame, settling down to it, 'that the English drink coffee in the middle of the mornings?'

'Oh yes, always.'

'In France never. Coffee for breakfast, yes, but then no food till lunch-time. And what exactly is a Coffee Morning? Marie-Claire tells me they are for charity.' She looked bewildered. 'For what charitable purpose then do you drink coffee?'

'Oh, Cruelty to Animals or Children, or Cancer or Multiple Sclerosis. Or even,' I added hastily, seeing her stupefaction, 'for Distressed Gentlewomen.' (What on earth was the French for Gentlewoman?)

'You drink coffee for animals?'

'To help to stop cruelty to animals, yes.'

'And children? To stop cruelty to children also?'

'Yes.' This was certainly a dark blot on our escutcheon. 'I'm afraid so.'

Monsieur then became intrigued. 'After you have drunk coffee, what then?'

'We just talk or we buy at the Bring and Buy stall.'

'Bring and Buy?' I explained the intricacies of this so English custom.

'Do gentlemen attend these coffee mornings?'

I thought hard. 'Occasionally; if they are retired.' I did remember an old gentleman of eighty coming to one of mine.

'I hear,' confided M'sieur with the air of playing a trump card, 'that in offices and factories they stop work to drink coffee in the mornings and tea in the afternoons?'

'That's true,' I said miserably thinking what a coffee-ridden lazy lot of layabouts the British workpeople must seem.

'But,' said James forcibly, downing his Calvados, 'our lunch break is only an hour and a quarter, and we have no siesta and NO SAINTS' DAYS.'

We had suffered badly from Saints' Days abroad, finding them an insuperable barrier to making appointments, or mending punctures or even shopping.

'I think,' said Madame soothingly, 'that the English women are good organisers and good committee women. Now we French are not given to committees. We organise within the family. How do you say, the iron hand in the velvet glove.'

'We will drink,' I said thickly, 'to the velvet glove.'

† † †

It was no real surprise to us that Jon gave up his lotos-eating life with Carpenter and came back to London, where Nicola was working while waiting to go to university.

At eleven o'clock one night I got a phone call from her, this time without reversing the charges which indicated something important was on hand. Could she and Jon come down on Sunday for Daddy's birthday? Would it be all right and would Daddy be there? No, Daddy wouldn't be there as he was in hospital with appendicitis, contracted two days after returning from France.

So Nicola and Jon went straight to the hospital here, carrying like a peace-offering a bottle of wine, and said to James in their first breath, 'Can we get engaged, please? Now?'

This is a difficult question to answer when you are just recovering from appendicitis. James played for time and finally suggested that they wait till Christmas. They were so relieved that he didn't actually oppose it that they demurred very little at the suggestion, but it seemed to me that it would be fitting for Nic to go up to university engaged or he might lose her and so we compromised on September.

July

Each year the French youngsters who come over have a current nickname for parents. The first year it was 'P.P.H.' ('passera pas l'hiver - won't last the winter'). The second time it was Les Ruines. Several times I was forcibly reminded that I was a Ruin, until the in-word here became 'a Square', and then James and I became squares. Not that James becomes violently anything in the eyes of the children as he treats all their urges and enthusiasms quite benignly, but Mum is a different matter.

I was a square because I held out very firmly against holiday jobs for the under-fourteens. I know now that they were, all of them, at the spearhead of a movement which has since established itself as normal, and I have learned too that once a social habit has caught on no castigation or inducement will deflect the teenager from following it. It is IN; they must do it. 'Twas ever thus,' quotes James complacently whenever I complain.

Their arguments with me became passionate for a time. 'You're just the complete square; everybody earns; we have needs just like you. Why should we be limited by parents' pocket-money? That isn't going to get us far.' True, in our family, very true.

I thought it over and now I am neither ruin nor square. I have given in. Not without some bargaining however. I stipulated that Roger set himself up with some clothes for his first job in September, and that Sue might earn part of her fare to France and either youngster could naturally keep what was over. Roger took a very dim view that clothing was in any way a necessity and wanted to save up for a vintage car. But commonsense prevailed. He hied himself to a furniture store in Norwich and got himself allocated to the delivery department; thus he spent a glorious fortnight touring the villages of Norfolk, knocking on farmhouse doors with rolls of linoleum. Occasionally he worked in the warehouse which wasn't so much fun, but which he liked because he could always nip a nap on a mattress.

But now he has moved to one of the vaults in our major insurance firm, all by himself on the top of a ladder sorting out old Financial Times. He finds this a bit dull after the delivery van and keeps nipping out to the coffee machine which, as a potential engineer, impresses him because it has buttons for black coffee, white coffee, sugar, no sugar; or tea with milk, without milk, sugar, no sugar...He stocks up each night with threepenny bits so heaven knows how much he drinks. Occasionally a girl ambles down to share his solitude. He reckons all the girls are pretty luscious upstairs and is therefore getting heartily tired of sorting out and solitude.

Next day he is moved on to files and the girls complain that they are often upside down.

'Wasn't me,' he says cheerfully. 'I found 'em that way and just put 'em back the same.'

Apart from these moronic activities he relates each day what he had for lunch in the canteen.

'Smashing,' he says.

Sue found a niche for herself picking fruit, a chore at which she was speedy and efficient. Thus each morning on the stroke of seven, before we squares had properly opened our eyes, the workers upped and packed their haversacks and went off to catch fruit lorry or delivery van.

On the question of Joanna I was still adamant. 'It isn't necessary to go out and earn money at your age (thirteen). What about me giving you some pocket-money to paint the bedroom? I need it doing desperately.'

'Not on. Boring. It's more profitable to earn outside.'

I might have won the day nevertheless if Sue hadn't come back from the fruit fields with news that at least half-a-dozen of Joanna's schoolmates were on the rows with her and going back for the rest of the week. So again I gave in.

Joanna however had found her own place to pick, advertised in the evening paper; lorry to leave city centre at 8.15 in the morning. At seven o'clock she and the others went through the ritual of packing lunch, filling up lemonade bottles, stuffing duffel bags, and went off to catch the lorries. At 9.30 Joanna came disconsolately home again. The lorry hadn't arrived and a hundred and fifty people were left stranded and she'd got so hungry she'd eaten her lunch, which she admitted was very tasty.

So the next morning she tried again, leaving an hour early in order to be first. And first she was, but not on the lorry. They wouldn't let her on; she wasn't a regular and wasn't with a parent; someone had borrowed her last sixpence for a fizzy orange so she walked two miles home. And this time she was too discouraged even to eat her hard-boiled eggs.

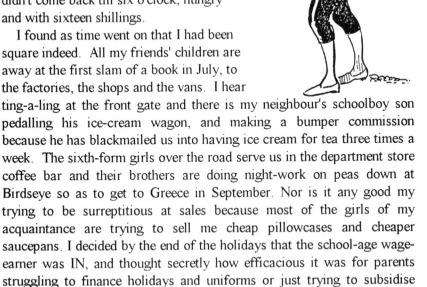

This last disappointment put up even my hackles. I rang up the field where Sue worked. Yes, they might be able to fit Joanna in if she would cycle the seven miles. So we packed her off again with a two-shilling piece for emergencies, the hardboiled eggs, a mackintosh and a kneeling-pad (we're experts on equipment), and this time she didn't come back till six o'clock, hungry and with sixteen shillings.

I found as time went on that I had been square indeed. All my friends' children are away at the first slam of a book in July, to the factories, the shops and the vans. I hear ting-a-ling at the front gate and there is my neighbour's schoolboy son pedalling his ice-cream wagon, and making a bumper commission because he has blackmailed us into having ice cream for tea three times a week. The sixth-form girls over the road serve us in the department store coffee bar and their brothers are doing night-work on peas down at Birdseye so as to get to Greece in September. Nor is it any good my trying to be surreptitious at sales because most of the girls of my acquaintance are trying to sell me cheap pillowcases and cheaper saucepans. I decided by the end of the holidays that the school-age wage-earner was IN, and thought secretly how efficacious it was for parents struggling to finance holidays and uniforms or just trying to subsidise present-day children. It could be that in a year or two parents would be quite expendable in the vacation. Or at any time? Sobering thought.

But perhaps not all young people are as self-sufficient as they seem.

Nicola had taken a job in London that was paid by the month. One night, in the middle of my preparations for workers in field and van, making corned beef sandwiches and setting jellies, the phone rang. Nic, breathing a fervent S.O.S.!

'Please wire me some money, Mummy; my salary hasn't arrived by post as they promised it would and I can't even rake up the train fare home. No, I can't borrow, 'cos everybody at the hostel's away for the weekend except me and I'm DESTITUTE!'

As we hurtled down to the G.P.O. I felt we were not quite such ruins after all. *Somebody* needed us.

August - and a wet weekend

There's something very cosy and satisfying about a Bank Holiday that ends in rain. You get rid of that aching feeling of wanting to grasp every minute just because it *is* Bank Holiday. You pull in the deck chairs and the bathing suits off the line (because nobody else will if you don't), and let down the tennis net and foregather in the living-room for tea and conversation. And as the wet evening wears on you light the lights although it is only August, progress from tea to coffee, watch the telly without feeling guilty at missing the sunshine, and go to bed early with a book.

This weekend has been such a one.

It has been very satisfying with all the teenagers home. Nic brought Jon, and Roger went round for Alex, and Judy over the road came anyway, and even Geoff, on leave from Ghana, came to fetch his children to spend a few days at his Kent home. Yesterday was all tennis and sunshine and salads and today, after a morning swim for the youngsters, rain and coffee and records, with Nic and Jon catching the 5.40 train back to London.

The remnants of the holiday lie like flotsam around the house: sand, towels and sandals, five pairs of tennis shoes in an unintentional rosette, sunglasses and plastic cups and racquets and washing-up, oceans of it. A long trail of flex snakes its way over the lawn where the radio extension was erected and a green hose coils its length outside the back door where Father anticipated that rain would never come. A soft drizzle sifts over everything, blotting out the shrubbery and blurring the dark edges of the flower-beds. Another Bank Holiday over.

There were eleven of us for most of the weekend. I made a large veal and ham pie and boiled a piece of collar bacon, baked a cherry cake and roasted a colossal piece of topside and it just about saw us through.

In the middle of the junketing we heard that Marilyn Monroe had died. Pity. Rather like the sun going in.

☨　☨　☨

This month too, I have, as Sue announced to the assembled company, reached a landmark in birthdays. I woke up to a card from Penny with an elephant on it and the legend, 'Let's face it, you're a year older,' and written round its rump, 'It sticks out a mile.' Underneath in pencil, 'No offence meant. Love Penny.'

Joanna is slightly more self-conscious. She was a bit doubtful about her card to me and showed it to me beforehand. It depicted a slim and beautiful girl with the wording:

> 'When it comes to your shape
> You may as well figger
> Before it gets smaller
> It's gonna get bigger.'

Possible yes, but not probable. Joanna agreed with me on second thoughts, but she had paid one and threepence for it. Perhaps it would do for Auntie Lynette, whose birthday (though not age) was the same as mine. I thought perhaps not. So we bought Lynette a substitute with ten baby bunnies on it, and stuck the picture of the siren in a drawer till the right pregnant lady turned up.

At crack of dawn the currant-pickers brought their offerings to my bed before they went: a pyrex dish, an enormous washing-up bowl, a crockery tea-set in fawn. Penny weighed in with two necklaces and Nana with a large damask dinner-cloth, God bless her.

But Sue had the last word. She gave me a sophisticated pack of talc and cologne. 'I wanted to get you "Love Affair",' she said, 'then I thought it wasn't really you, so I got "Frenzy".'

☨　☨　☨

January 1963 and the Great Freeze

I think this deserves a heading as it will probably go down in history. It certainly has in the annals of Eaton End. The Freeze started on December 22nd and through Christmas and the New Year we thought it just a cold snap, but since then it has mercilessly gone ON and ON and is now in its fourth week. Most of the time we just freeze, down to fingers and toes. We shovel snow, we light paraffin stoves because we have no anthracite (nobody has had, for three weeks). We are without water because the mains are frozen below ground and we are therefore thrown back on archaic forms of heating unused by us for years, like paraffin, logs and occasionally a haybox. We still, thank heaven, have a gas stove that works but no water to heat on it. The house, strange to say, is warmer than it has been for weeks, so afraid are we that it will become less so. I have fed eleven people most of the holidays in spite of insuperable difficulties, and am now expert at making and freezing a mousse in half-an-hour (for we have no fridge), the answer being to immerse it in snow. So hard is the freeze that the little oblong indentation in the wallflower bed where I put the dish each day is permanent. I could go to it in the dark. All this culinary activity is essential because Christmas has lasted roughly a fortnight; only now, mid-January, have Jon Chapple and Nic gone their various ways, and Roger started at the Technical College, where at least he'll be fed some lunch.

We have been like busy little ants: as soon as one catastrophe is righted we set to work on another. When the anthracite failed we sawed up hundreds of billets of wood to feed the solid fuel stove. For three weeks we sawed and shovelled them in until swags of soot festooned the stove, and bark and sawdust smothered the back step.

When the hot water tank froze we climbed daily three storeys with a Tilley lamp to thaw the pipes. Now we're covering the same ground with a bucket parade because the main pipes have frozen under the drive, and we're filling the hot tank with cold water to heat up for morning wash. Each day at 7.30 a.m. the family is summoned by Father to fill buckets at the cold bath on the first floor and join the parade. They comply with groans and grizzles for the route to the loft is cold and dusty, and they have to weave round the huge TV aerial and the drunken piles of suitcases in a manner reminiscent of Steptoe and Son.

How easily the crust of civilisation cracks. Have a water main freeze

and a power cut and you are back fifty years. The only safe bets are a log fire and a well in the backyard. This is the winter of the he-man and superwoman, the sawer of wood and drawer of water. If you can find the water. By some quirk of nature our own underground mains are frozen solid while my neighbours' outside stand-pipe is flowing freely. They are charitable and allow us to use it. It is sixty feet across a lawn and through a hedge and I wade through the snow to attach the hosepipe to it, rush back upstairs to the bathroom to monitor the flow into the bath, wait till it is three-quarters full and rush across the lawn again to turn off. Every day. Sometimes there is a variation: I fill a few downstairs utensils too. Clustered round my washer are a bucket, a Victorian jug, two preserving pans and a tin bath. I fill these, swoosh, swoosh, and heaven help me if the grocer arrives or the milkman suddenly wants paying in which case I swoosh, swoosh the floor as well.

And yet... There are, in all the hassle, some very pleasing moments, like bathing in hot melted snow in front of the kitchen stove; with small leaves a-floating, the corpses of tiny red wrigglers drifting and the soft caress of snow-water on the skin. The cares of the day fall away. It takes me back to my childhood, to the zinc bath in front of the scullery copper, before we got the water-heater upstairs, and to the matiness that emergencies bring when everyone is in the same boat. But later at night, warm from our make-do heating, watching a good programme on TV, it does seem a bit hard to go back to all that cold-water-carrying in the morning. Believe me, when the first trickle comes through the tap again we'll be celebrating in champagne. *And* it won't be watered down!

‡ ‡ ‡

171

February

And then came The Party.

'There'll be about sixty coming,' Roger had said. 'There's nothing you need do except provide a barrel of beer. And perhaps cheese thingummies and a cake. When we run out of beer they can bring their own. It's quite usual. We shan't need you, except to pay for the beer barrel. Just leave us to it.'

My first thought was that it would be a mighty big cake that would go round sixty and it would take a fair number of cheese thingummies also, but I promised to make both, and after that, lulled into a sense of serenity that proved false, we left Roger to the rest of the arrangements.

A little nearer the date he said casually: 'Some people's parents go out and leave them the house, you know.'

I had a smart reply to that. Where did he think seven of us were going even if we agreed, which we didn't? We promised to go up into Nana's bedroom and watch the telly. Would that do? This placated Roger.

On the night itself, the beer barrel and sixty glasses being established in the sun room and the cake in the lounge, we retired as promised. In the end there were only five of us as Sue and Joanna wanted to join in the revels downstairs. We settled down to 'Sunday Night at the Palladium'.

About half-past seven the fun started. The first car doors started slamming in the drive and a gentle buzz rose up from the hall; in minutes the buzz became a roar and young people arrived by every door. Outside in the street, the driveway being jammed, cars, vans and bicycles piled up.

A rich haze of cigarette smoke arose inside and reached us in the bedroom, the party being now well under way. Glasses clinked, records began to blare, laughter bellowed, girls shrieked. A mysterious sense of pressure began to assail us upstairs, for ours is a high narrow house, and we got the impression that the walls were about to burst outwards. On investigating through a crack in the door we saw that the tide of guests had flowed up the stairs and on to the landing and more were arriving every minute. Gradually a queue formed outside our very bedroom, but by subtle enquiry we found that was for the loo.

'There's another upstairs,' we said, trying to be helpful, and immediately another queue started there.

By ten o'clock, feeling like a member of a besieged garrison, I decided to forage for coffee. I bulldozed a passage through the stair squatters.

They looked at me incuriously as strangers do, politely hitched sideways and stubbed out their cigarettes in the plant pots. I excused my way to the kitchen. Here the light had failed and shadowy couples were making the most of the darkness. Feeling the worst kind of intruder on this so intimate scene I apologised to a couple glued together by the larder and with trembling hands put the kettle on and collected some food. A face appearing in the dimness coalesced into the features of the boy across the road. His was the only one I recognised in the whole milling crowd. He took my tray and fought a way for me back to the stairs.

There were then about sixty people in the lounge and sun-room and fifteen on the stairs and landings. Another twenty were jam-packed in the dining-room and still folk were coming and going by every entrance. Those in the rooms, particularly in the centre, stood in a solid wodge unable to move, tasting the high life on two glasses of beer, a flood of cigarette butts gently deepening round their feet for no-one could move to reach an ash-tray. Conversations took place over each other's heads. Togetherness was tops.

At midnight we decided to show some resistance. Most of the lights were out and what was happening was anybody's guess. James took charge and winkled out Roger who appeared cheerfully from somewhere, quite euphoric. 'Don't worry, Dad, the party's dwindling. They're going on to someone else.' (Good luck to the someone else, I thought.) He must have given some ritualistic sign for gradually there was a general unhooking movement, a brushing-down of skirts and jeans, a patting of hair and a fair amount of giggling and on the whole a movement towards the door. As the fresh air hit them they flinched, but most of them turned round and thanked us charmingly, almost surprised to find there was someone over twenty present who, possibly, owned the house.

In ten minutes the battlefield was clear. We looked around. In all honesty we could not recognise our large front room as the one we had left at eight o'clock. A grey cloud had settled alike on furniture and chattels. There was, I reckoned quite soberly, an eighth of an inch sheared off the carpet pile, even though there hadn't been much to start with. Cigarette stubs and packets just lay around. Beer bottles and dirty glasses jostled each other on every horizontal surface including the stair treads. An amber pool oozed from under the barrel along the sun-room floor. The wastepaper basket was riddled with burn-holes. We rolled up our sleeves, got out the vacuum cleaner, mops and dusters and set to.

'Fab party,' said Roger, 'the only one in the city tonight ackcherly, except for the one run by the nurses up the road.' (So that was where they all went.) 'We've had the lot tonight, the whole jolly lot. A hundred and forty! Really fab.' He added as an afterthought: 'Usually the place gets broken up, we were lucky.'

I aimed half a beer glass into the burnt wastepaper basket. 'Very lucky,' said I.

October

Autumn again and the last teenager has gone off to school or technical college or university and the glory has departed. Nic went to Liverpool University yesterday and the boy friends, girl friends, chatter and innumerable cups of coffee have evaporated till Christmas. Even the huge brass rubbing of Sir Roger de Trumpington that has stared at us all impassively in the living-room over the holidays has gone; rolled up and despatched to decorate a bedsitter in Liverpool. I shall miss him as I shall miss many things.

I had thought to bid Nic a tender goodbye on the station platform in true mother and daughter fashion as she went off to lead her new independent life, but I was wrong. Half an hour before she left, the gang arrived - Jeremy of coypu fame and one or two girl friends. They humped her trunks down two flights of stairs, swallowed several cups of coffee apiece and piled into the battered car. Instructions from Nic buzzed around my head: 'I've left the trunks in the hall. Give the British Rail man five and sixpence and tear the bit off the form and send it to me. And send me extra sheets - though really I don't need two pairs; I can wash these out and use them again...'

'You can't, you can't...'

'Yes I can, hot-air dryers. And a pillow, don't forget the pillow. Here's my address, write it down quick. It's temporarily a Mrs. Bullivant, but after that we get a flat and I'll LET YOU KNOW...'

This last was bawled on the wind. The gang waved, there was a flurry of leaves in the drive and she was gone.

† † †

I came to, gently, surveying the wreckage. The hall was full of trunks. The telephone was surrounded by messages, stuck at all angles, scribbled on old programmes, notices, cards. 'Mike will fetch you 7.15.' 'Tell Hugh I arrive Liverpool 6.40.' (Hugh? Hugh? What about Jon?) 'RAISINS.' 'Can she stay with your aunt if not the Y.W.?' And one that is too practical to belong to Nic, but is probably James's: 'Gravel 28/- cu. yd.'

I climbed the stairs to the second floor. The bedroom was full of sweet smells, drifts of powder, cartons of hair bleach, love-letters left casually around, sunglasses, switches of hair, and C. P. Snow's 'Strangers and Brothers'. With only the faintest sigh I started to clear up. An hour later I dipped my hand into my apron pocket and found a dog-eared shopping list:

> 6 lbs. loaf sugar
> 1 doz. Kilner rings

Two stones of ripening pears to be bottled! Once again I bent my mind towards the chores.

† † †

Nic has rung up (reverse charges of course) from Liverpool to say she had a MARVELLOUS flat, only seven pounds a week and could I send two sheets, two blankets and an eiderdown, and a pillow if I could afford the postage; and the transparencies of the holidays were MARVELLOUS and she was having prints made. I know she can't afford the flat or the prints, but what's the use...?

The next communication was by letter, apparently she was able to afford a stamp. After alarms over the flat the landlord has sued her for three weeks' rent in lieu of notice, and she has since capsized in the Mersey and clung for twenty minutes to the overturned boat. While I was subconsciously visualising the pollution there might be in the Mersey and whether she had had the staying power to hang on to the boat, I read on about the suing business. Apparently the landlord promised the flat to two groups of tenants, and Nic's lot, having the ready money for the first month, got it. The previous group, arriving with bedding, were fobbed off. When the university heard about it they forbade Nic and company to stay there, allowing them just the week and then siphoning them off into digs. The landlord promptly sued for the remaining three weeks. The university are defending it. I read this with a kind of armchair satisfaction. It's nice to know someone else is standing in loco parentis.

† † †

Letter from Sue to Nicola at university:

'School is absolutely mouldy, but at least we are now allowed to do our homework there and they are providing a cup of tea - we don't have to pay! Daddy sends his love to you and says he is failing fast. Joanna is still the worst girl in the school, leading the class into scrapes. Roger is saving up for an Alvis Firefly, no money yet but he's going in for every Mini-Minor competition possible to try and get a car that way. I went to the Young Farmers' Dance last week. Good fun but the boys won't dance.' I feel this sums up the current situation pretty neatly.

† † †

Penny comes cheerfully in from school. 'I've got something to tell you, something to ask you and something to show you. We've won the netball, every game, 4L that is; and can I have 2/6d. off my next week's pocket money to go to "Summer Holiday" and the thing I've got to show you is *this*.' She holds out gingerly a light package wrapped in newspaper.

I unwrap it gently, first the newspaper, then the greaseproof. A large bull's eye glares at me unwinkingly.

'I bought it for biology, off a stall in the market. And Sandra's got the other one. We're going to dissect it tomorrow,' and off she trots, button eyes glowing.

The next night she returns with a very satisfied look on her face. 'We dissected the bull's eye. First we jabbed it and all jelly stuff came out, squirt! Then we dissected the eyeball. Then we turned the eyeball inside out to look at the nerves. Then we investigated the eyestalk. Gorgeous.'

† † †

James was right. University proved too heady to sustain Nic's engagement. Some time after the Great Freeze she and Jon broke up. I'm sure the end must have been difficult, taking place as it did at a halfway house between Liverpool and London. It was the first real emotional involvement in the family and I think we all learned from it a little.

February 1964

Nana is eighty-seven this month and has recovered well from a rather nasty physical setback, a broken blood-vessel in her stomach, and for a day or two she was quite ill with a haemorrhage. Her digestion was upset, her skin became dry and yellow like parchment, and she continued at intervals to retch. Slowly, however, she won through.

The doctor thinks she is indestructible. He gave her some analgesic suppositories to stop the retching.

'They'll make her feel drowsy,' he said, 'and probably knock her out. They're pretty strong. They'll also have the usual suppository effect.'

They had no effect whatever except to give her hallucinations. She complained that her pension book kept going square and that things disappeared when she went to pick them up. As for a suppository effect, bunkum.

The doctor stood on the front step as he left and marvelled.

'Incredible,' he said, 'at 87. They'd have knocked a normal person for six. She's tough, your mother.'

Yes, we'd gathered that. But better that way, perhaps.

The birthday is imminent and I've had the doubtfully pleasant task of suggesting an all-over special wash, with perhaps some nice talc to finish off with. But when I suggest anywhere below the belt I meet with opposition.

'It's me shoulder-blades I want doing, where I broke them.' She had fallen under a lorry once, on her bicycle. 'I can't reach them with this arm,' and she vigorously waves the arm around her head area, meanwhile pulling her nightgown well up round her neck.

'There's a back brush beside you,' said I, the irritation beginning to rise because it wasn't the shoulders I was after.

'I can't manage a back brush, can't reach the spot.'

'It's curved,' I point out hopefully. 'Got a long handle.' No use. So I start on her back.

'Plenty of soap,' she commands. I resoap the flannel already soaped and overflow surreptitiously under the arms and round the ribs.

'I can *do* the front,' she orders sharply, 'don't want the front doing. I want a good hard scrub between the shoulder-blades.'

We each know exactly what we are about, my mother and I, each parrying the other. I give her a second scrub between the shoulders, and later try to work downwards.

'Don't want washing down there. I can reach there meself. It's just me shoulders,' and back we go to the same spot. I rescrub a third time and throw a towel over her.

'Rub hard so that it glows,' came a muffled voice from under the night-gown. I rub, I shake on some powder. Evidently the feel of it reminds her that she'd like some.

'Put some of that nice powder on,' says she, and then, 'Lovely, lovely, now I can do the front,' and I am dismissed.

I make use of the dismissal, sneak into her bedroom, grab the sweeper and make inroads on the cottons and crumbs while the sound of the tap is drowning my activity. She catches me at it, grabs her red hat reproachfully and says, 'There'll be dust all over me hat. I always put it right away before I start sweeping.' But let us not quibble. We have managed three-quarters of a blanket bath, victory enough for one day.

It turned out in the end a Really Good Do. Nana played hostess to all her cronies, Mrs Warner, the oldest, being ninety-four and the youngest Dr Isabel Brodie, Nana's niece, one of the Scottish Chalmers clan. And of course Percy, my nature curist, who brought a bottle of his own tea wine with a twinkle in his eye and a spring in his step, for at eighty he had just won a medal for ballroom dancing. The room itself was redolent of a florist's shop, alive with spring flowers and here and there a box of chocolates. We unearthed Grandma's gilded tea-cups, the Limoges plates hand-painted with geraniums and Nana's silver tea-set. We crowned the festivities with a birthday cake in pink and white icing, result of much sweat and deliberation.

Poor Percy sat there isolated by his deafness watching the antics of the ladies, Isabel being on her knees most of the time trying to work out Nana's family tree. Grandma Chalmers had sewn a sampler in eighteen fifty something but as the years passed on and she wasn't married she picked out the last figure in the birthdate and no one quite knew what it had been. It hangs on our wall now; 'Isabella Chalmers sewed this sampler at seven years old in 185-'.

Nana loved it all, cards cake, greeting telegrams, flowers, the lot - a small oasis of Edwardiana in the middle of the twentieth century. Will my generation produce as lively a côterie in their eighties and nineties? I wonder.

Late December

Today I feel I must write again about Nana, not quite as indestructible as she seemed. In the last year she has been having a series of setbacks, part of the process of wearing out; arthritis worsening in the hip (a bad gnawing pain), a stomach ulcer, incontinence, stone in bladder, and failing sight in an operated eye. Now her salivary glands are ceasing to work. She complained of a dry mouth and began to suck rather than eat her food, the saliva collecting behind her throat. Over Christmas with all the youngsters home, she would retire for exhausting spitting sessions, painstakingly and neatly coughing, spitting and wiping in a way that would break anyone else's spirit. Sometimes I would wake up after an hour's nap to find her still there, patiently wiping away.

We put her on a liquid diet, soup, complan and ice cream and in three weeks she looked like someone out of Belsen, her tough sinewy body and like mind having taken a terrible beating. Her legs and feet swelled and broke innumerable little veins that purpled her left foot. The diuretic tablets given her to reduce this swelling only increased the incontinence. The resulting bed-wetting worried her and she called out about it in her sleep. We are really on a knife edge to keep the balance of liquid going in and out. Old age is not dignified.

1965

We are now through January. The build up of saliva mercifully has ceased without our really noticing. She is very weak, gradually beginning to leave us mentally and roam in a fantasy world. This is most noticeable night and morning when she is alone with me. When visitors come she revives. Our faithful Hannah who has been with us since Marina left is an invaluable help. I don't know what we would do without the Hannahs of this world.

In spite of these crises today has been a field day in the form of a National Council of Women meeting in the lounge. I joined the meeting while Hannah looked after her and afterwards her old pals paid their respects. So, perhaps for the last time, she held court, the twinkle back in her eye, the energy somehow dredged up from the depths.

In the middle of the afternoon a well-dressed lady appeared with an enormous bouquet of spring flowers. 'From Spain.' I did some quick thinking, the Spanish connection was usually Chris and Jane, Geoff's brother and his wife who all those years ago had offered to adopt Penny.

179

The smiling messenger was a Torremolinos neighbour. Chris and Jane who, since they retired to Spain, seldom managed to visit Norwich, will never know how opportune their flowers were. To Nana they were like an early birthday celebration, the one that should take place next month, but which I doubt she will ever see.

February 7th

The great battle is over. Nana died early yesterday. Her struggle with life and ours with her are resolved. The loving/contentious relationship has somehow finished with love. I suspected it was there all the time, overlaid with a fierce independence and little vanities and a great desire not to give in. It was the old struggle for personal recognition. I know it, I know it well.

For five days after the meeting she had shown a great decline. The morning after it I found her in bed with a pillow over her bare shoulders. She had struggled to remove a wet nightgown and with terrific strength had torn the neck. The mental effect of this wrenching must have been considerable, and she was never really with us from that day. She said several times, 'This is the end, isn't it? This is the finish.' In the face of such clarity one felt defenceless. She then said goodbye to everyone in turn, including my father and her first husband, William, and some good neighbours, and thanked me in words that I won't write here, and after that it was mostly cloudiness with odd returns to consciousness from very far away whenever anyone called her name. One of the last to speak with her was Roger. She had previously sold her gold watch to buy him a tool for his impending engineering career. He came in, cheerful as usual, bearing a plane. The grey eyes flickered. 'Good,' she said, 'good. Use it well;' and the fantasy world claimed her again...

Long after she had stopped taking any liquids her heart battled on, but after two days of coma, it too, ceased.

The main feature of Nana's death was the great kindness everyone showed in their admiration of her. She would have enjoyed her obituary notices. In the Daily Telegraph she ranked with a Countess, a Lady and a Knight, and gained a hyphen to boot, Mrs Agnes Marshall-Loomes. What is more the local papers called her a pioneer, 'one of the first women in England to be appointed Magistrate' and also 'one of the pioneers, in this country, of Infant Welfare Centres'. Yes, she would have appreciated that, would have been tickled pink in fact.

On my return I wander round clearing up Nana's small store of worldly goods (her silver, her jewellery and the antique furniture all having been given to us years ago). I dust her wheelchair for collection by the social services, sort her papers, scrub at last her room with its large portrait of my father with the jessamine in his buttonhole; put away her important little shortbread tin where she kept her biscuits and her serviette and her big box of photos dating back to Whitelands College, including a fingered copy of 'Fors Clavigera' 1898, the Ruskin Prize at the May Queen Festival, awarded to Agnes Gray 'because she believes in deeds rather than words'. A fitting epitaph.

February 23rd

And after the peaceful death the violent irrational one. Hannah disappeared a week ago, walked out as she had done once before, her house spotless, the fire lit and no money in her pocket. So where is she now? In what ditch is she lying or against what riverbank is she dashed? The afternoon she left Tom and her terraced house there was a biting frost and today there is snow so that her body would be blanketed from the naked eye, Hannah, so small that a puff of wind would blow her away, Hannah in her high black boots and her best blue coat and her blue-and-gold headscarf.

It is possible that Nana's death was the last straw plus the fact that I had gone away for a rest and the house was empty all day. Hannah had her own domestic traumas and Nana and I were a form of bedrock. But the heaviest straws were provided by husband Tom when he bought a house at auction, without a survey. The new house proved to be damp, had no special heating, was already converted into two flats and needed £4000 to put right. He then resold it to 'some foreigners', and found rightly or wrongly that Hannah and he would have to live in it instead to avoid capital gains tax.

It was when surrounded by all the boxes ready to move that something must have snapped in Hannah's brain. She had already been without heating the whole week because of North Sea Gas conversion; they were going to have to cook on a picnic stove in the new place and then I suddenly rang to say I was going away.

The day after this the snow came, heavy, blinding, sifting down as a white blanket over the Barnard household and variously obliterating two of its erstwhile occupants. But where *is* Hannah?

181

March 15th

Hannah was lying in the mud in the slipway at Wroxham - black boots turned to brown, kid gloves neatly on, blue-and-yellow headscarf tied, just as the papers said and as Tom identified her. Her face was swollen and scratched where the water had buffeted it. Three weeks.

The police think she had not been in the water all that time. Probably she went straight to the river that frosty night and was washed up later into the mud. No one would notice her in mud; it covered her face and probably most of her body. It is no use trying to be imaginative or emotional about what happened that night. Hannah went straight to death as unerringly as a death wish could take her.

‡   ‡   ‡

There are certain fallacies about the publicity of missing people. For one thing the flashing smiling face under the wedding hat that appeared in the papers was not a true description of the Hannah that went out at dusk that February afternoon. Anyone looking for her would have seen a plodding little figure, darkly dressed, headscarf pulled tight, face tense, an invisible woman whom dozens must have seen and not seen, walking her way to Wroxham. Tom had also said that on the morning of her going he had left her in good spirits. But she hadn't been so for months. She just became quieter and quieter, and had not come to work for two days. So she didn't really talk normally to him that morning.

It is ironic that Nana and Hannah (who was an hysteric) got their publicity when it was too late to enjoy it.

‡   ‡   ‡

April 1965

However Spring and optimism are here again and it is time I did some catching up on the home front.

We have now moved on from the bike era to the car era, mercifully missing out motorcycles but inevitably adding girl friends to the heaps of scrap-iron dotting the garden. Each, it seems, attracts the other.

Every day during weekends and holidays there are two to four cars, mostly other people's, in the long drive leading to our wooden garages, Roger's old Alvis (in pieces), his pal David's (in one piece), Nic's latest boy friend's second-hand Rover, put together largely from the junkyard, and when possible James's Westminster. James, usually the last comer-in, has to queue up even to reach the garage area, where there now isn't room to turn between the ironware. He also has to back out all the way down the drive, negotiating with care the bend by the walnut tree. This is not always achieved without hazard; on one occasion he encountered Roger's bike sticking out of the privet hedge, got out to move it leaving the car in gear so that it jumped, jammed the bike, and wrenched off part of the car door. This added another bash to the long pattern of dents already there, including mine, for I am now an embryo driver, though more prone to knocking down the back porch than other people's cars. Sue is learning too, so I suggested Dad left the beating-out process until she had added her quota, but dear old Sue is so level-headed that I fear any additional dents will not be hers.

Joanna is due to go to a dance but unfortunately the current hamster has imposed his machinations on her machinations and eaten the bottom off her skirt. She keeps its cage in her bedroom next to the chest of drawers. After a few hors-d'oeuvres of James's pyjamas, Roger's dress shirt and the bed-curtains, it pulled Joanna's skirt into its cage and chomped the hem off it. I thought myself that that was just retribution for being confined to a bedroom, but the owner's tears, cussing and first-aid repairs have been going on all day just as if Hammy had done it for spite. We put up a new hem and that made the thing too short even as a hipster skirt, so, reluctantly, she had to go to the dance in her grey woollen. This rather put her out of the running as the most way-out dresser of the gang, the top-notch gear to beat being black polo-necked sweater with open-necked denim shirt on top, denim skirt, tartan stockings and long brown boots.

And talking about gear, Janet, quite competitive in her own line, heard that Geoff, back in England, had acquired a new boat, and she bought a gurt shiny blue wet-look mackintosh, a sou'wester and a pair of boots, with her eye on sailing in them, thinking she might look like Cathy Gale perhaps, but only really succeeding, said the others, in looking like a postman on a wet day. It was sad for her that Geoff had already picked his crew to sail to France, but he gave Janet a joy-ride as far as Folkestone, from which she took a train home.

But knowing Janet the gear will come in useful. Already she and Penny are talking of taking a boat on the Broads one year. Good for them.

And we are always surrounded by the Beatles (this year Long Tall Sally, A Hard Day's Night). When it isn't their rhythms pulsating from radios and records all over the house it is the Rollers, or Cliff and the Shadows or the Supremes or the Animals or Manfred Mann or...you name 'em, we've got 'em.

Roger, after some vicissitudes, is apprenticed to an electronic engineering firm, which leaves him so much time to spare that he retires behind the machines to relax. One evening he came home exhausted and lay flat out on the sofa. Such a hard day, said he, deadpan. He'd read an entire novel, 'Women under the Shadow', all about lesbians. (Good heavens, I thought, I didn't know what a lesbian was till I was thirty.)

'What on earth made you buy that?'

'Oh, some bloke left it on the test bed,' said he. Sounds like the great electronic engineering book club!

One of his pals tells us that the supervisor discovered him laid out behind the machines one day and demanded what the blank he thought he was doing.

'Well,' drawled Roger, 'I was actually trying to have a nap.'

From where, I wonder, does he get this devastating honesty?

I have now entered Public Life in a small way and it is essential that I drive a car. Public Life is taking me to Ipswich and various villages in the county to Speak, or to conferences, some of it in order to be trained as a Responsible Citizen, helping other citizens to be responsible also.

So some days I wake up with considerable apprehension because I have a driving lesson and Mr Plumb is very precise, one might even say pernickety. He won't let me vary any procedure to suit my particular personality, which is perhaps just as well, though his predecessor allowed it and I was much more relaxed. I give quick looks right and left at crossroads and he doesn't notice that I have given any at all; in fact my reactions are too quick altogether but my gear changes not quick enough. However one day he took his sunglasses off and I was able to see how much like Cary Grant he was, less remote and Buddha-like, which endeared me slightly. Perhaps, after all, his needling is because of his pupil: I must be a trial at times.

But it seems I am not yet a Responsible Driver, as there is no mention of a test. I look with envy at the delivery men and seventeen-year-olds in rusty bangers and wonder what they have that I haven't. Caution at crossroads, says Mr Plumb.

June

Sue and Joanna are taking A-level and O-level exams respectively this year, Penny having already taken O's. Sue, as always an equable influence in the family, is going to Warwick University in October. Joanna has come a long way along a somewhat different path. She continued to be the worst girl in the school for quite some years, a period that I bore with exasperation and Father with amused tolerance. Whenever he wanted to give her some fatherly advice he withdrew to the sitting-room and had a one-to-one session behind my disapproving back. Rebel to rebel, no doubt. But at last one can see signs of femininity emerging in the tomboy make-up, like a struggling rose in a wasteland. Her bedroom is full of nail varnishes and remover, make-up and cleansers for that perfect skin, mascara and eye-shadow for those long blonde lashes, and bracelets, earrings and scarves, for everywhere else; and of course dresses. I have counted as many as fifteen pairs of shoes. In fact all her spare money goes on clothes and records and we are working through the Beatles, though I see signs of them becoming passé already.

At the last painting of the bedroom (Nic's old attic) we took down the picture and cuttings gallery. Around Terence Stamp who had pride of place were several torn-out items of news, some stuck in the mirror, some sellotaped on the wall. 'FIVE-MINUTE MIRACLE,' announced the biggest:

'1. Smooth a honey toned base liquid over face and neck for an all-over even glow that covers up minor imperfections but allows the skin to show through...magically.

2. Glaze the eyelids with the tiniest glimmer of eye-gloss that will make your lids shimmer even in the darkest corners of a disco.

3. Slick the most subtle glow on your cheek cushions, and contour it by sucking in your cheeks and patting blusher in the hollowed centres.

4. Glaze your mouth with sheer colour for the newest lip look; smooth with your finger for come-hither-ness.'

Beside this legend was a cut-out of a long lean juvenile delinquent girl slouched against a graffiti-ed wall; and written beneath:

'Sling over a slinky shirt of Irish coffee a woolly Sloppy Joe cardigan in clearest Irish Whiskey, topping lager-coloured straight-leg trews buttoned down the fly front. Final pep, an earth-shaded chiffon scarf knotted cowboy-style round your slender neck.'

So that was where all the fruit-picking money went.

On the other side of the wardrobe mirror was stuck a rather neater excerpt, cut carefully with scissors:

'Charity is patient, kind: charity envieth not, dealeth not
    perversely, is not puffed up.
Is not ambitious, seeketh not her own, is not provoked to anger,
    thinketh no evil.....
Beareth all things, believeth all things, hopeth all things,
    endureth all things.....'

Body and soul, soul and body: the schizophrenia of youth.

‡ ‡ ‡

186

July - DEGREE DAY

In one of Liverpool's grottiest areas James and I stood on the doorstep of a house that had seen better days. I wore my shocking pink hat and James his best pin-stripes. Together in the Liverpool downpour, we looked like a couple of tropical fish in a puddle. Along the row of dilapidated Victorian houses the paint was peeling and the railings broken. Next door a woman sat on the steps and eyed us dully. Number twenty-three housed a collection of impecunious students like Nicola, just living above subsistence level, a state that went well with the district. We looked around for a knocker and, not finding one, pulled heftily on an old bell. It clanged lugubriously and the door suddenly opened to reveal a figure in a blue dressing-gown and outsize curlers.

'Oh, it's you!' cried Nicola in a surprised-relieved kind of voice. 'Goodness, it can't be as late as that! I've been up since seven and haven't had breakfast yet. Come in, I'll have to bang the door, there's no handle.' She banged it. We entered a dilapidated hall choc-a-bloc with trunks, hers and several others by the look of it.

'This is my room. Excuse the broken door panel, we had to force it one day. Look, I must go upstairs and wash: make yourselves at home. Perhaps you could finish my packing. Everything's got to go in the car except those boxes and they belong to the next tenant. He's coming in this evening,' and she disappeared, mules clacking, up the bare wood stairs.

We gazed around. It was difficult to know where to start. Seats and table were piled with clothes, dirty cups, books, a bird cage, a bookcase, blankets and cushions. A large plaster cast of false teeth and a bottle of Nuits St. George decorated the mantelpiece. An outsize Bernard Buffet print occupied the bed.

'Well,' volunteered James, 'I vote we start with the bookcase,' and he picked it up in both arms and staggered towards the front door. I turned to deal with the rest of the gear when a voice from somewhere up the stairs yelled, 'Mum, could you make me some coffee? Kitchen's at the back, mind the step.'

So I stepped out gingerly into the Victorian gloom and fell into the filthiest kitchen I have ever seen. On an encrusted stove stood a half-empty saucepan of milk; tins of coffee and impersonal nourishment like vinegar and salt stood about generally. Of proper food there was no sign. The whole room gave on to a small yard littered with papers. I gathered together milk, matches and instant coffee and brewed a cup of it which I took up to the bathroom.

'Come in,' said an abstracted voice. This was difficult to do as the bathroom was microscopic. On the bare floor was last Sunday's newspaper, strategically placed both to serve as carpet and to provide light reading whilst the occupant was otherwise engaged. A notice headed IMPORTANT gave instructions for preventing the geyser from blowing up. The toilet roll was in the soap dish and the soap was missing. A dark grey tidemark encircled the bath. Nicola, quite impervious to all this, was creating a gradual metamorphosis; the curlers were out, eyelashes were on, and with mouth wide she was carefully tracing a line with a lipbrush.

'Where do you want the coffee?' I asked rather helplessly. But as she could only make indeterminate noises I left the cup in the bath and withdrew downstairs.

James was still luggage-removing. 'Give me a hand with this steamer trunk,' he called over. 'I think we could jam it in the back of the car. The boot's full of birdcage.'

'Don't you think we could discreetly ditch the birdcage?' It used to contain two Java temple birds until one of them fell behind the old-fashioned wainscoting and was seen no more and the other flew out of the window. A voice from above called, 'No you don't. I'm going to breed budgies in it one day. You can find a corner for it somewhere.' I looked up to expostulate and then stopped short, for a moment non-plussed. On the stairs stood a complete transformation of the Nic I had seen in the bathroom, made up (literally) to the eyebrows, light hair swinging, soberly clad in a white blouse and dark subfusc skirt which seemed to emphasise more strongly the sparkle above.

I muttered something complimentary.

'Yes, thank you, but the skirt should really be black and the blouse up to the neck but this is all I've got. We have to be there at ten, so I must dash now, but you'd better come too or you won't find the way.'

She put down her tepid cup of coffee untouched and dashed over to the wardrobe.

'This place is riddled with mice which is rather nerve-racking, but a veterinary student gave me poison to get rid of them and that was even worse because I found baby mice dead all over the floor. Anyway,' with splendid unconcern, 'it'll be the next lodger's headache tonight. Now have you packed everything?'

'All but the false teeth and the Bernard Buffet.'

'Leave the teeth, they belong to the dental student next door. Impression of her favourite patient. Oh, come on, Mum, stop looking baffled. Let's go.' We went.

We were much too early of course and sat in the Philharmonic Hall up among the classical friezes for what seemed hours, watching the parents trickle in, most of the mothers wearing frothy special-occasion hats, just like me. Degree Day obviously goes to the head. We marvelled that Nicola's name was in the lists at all, after three years of crises too numerous to mention and enteritis in the middle of finals. Up there in the warm layer under the roof we relaxed and became nostalgic. James dreamed himself back thirty years to the Sheldonian at Oxford where degree day had been for him also the culmination of three very formative years. No doubt he was thinking himself back to the quad at John's and the springing turf of the Iffley Road playing-fields where he hurdled in for the university, and to the girl next door in the Cowley Road to whom he got engaged in those racing undergraduate days.

And I? Of what do mothers dream? Of a small lifetime of cherishing, I suppose. Of infectious diseases at home and heartbreaks at school. Of innumerable loved animals from hamsters to horses that drew on some reservoir of affection waiting to be tapped; of Beatrix Potter and Dr. Spock, and the Famous Five and Sacha Distel and the Beatles; and of all the young men in Nicola's particular case who breathed undying devotion, the Jons and Jeremys and Williams and Peters, and the faint air of perfume always drifting in her wake....

Somewhere about halfway Nicola appeared on the rostrum, a slight figure with thin wrists emerging from a too-large gown, mortar-board on shining hair: the end-product of twenty-two years of heartsearching, member of the new meritocracy, inheritor of the earth.

As she stepped into the circle of light, looking so young and vulnerable, I felt as mothers must have felt since the beginning of time, stabbed by an unexpected pride mingled with affection and delight, and, let's face it, with more than a tendency to tears. After all we'd been through a lot together, one way and another.

Up there in the half-light I felt for James's hand. Degree Day obviously goes to the heart too.

189

Christmas 1965

I still write as the spirit moves me but a feeling has come over me that Nic's degree was a milestone in our domestic life, the end of the beginning. Is this perhaps time to stop? Or to start again: new book, new era? Musing over this, I draw a heavy line under 1965.

But Penny, reading as usual over my shoulder, asks somewhat belligerently, 'Why finish here, Mum? There must be lots more to come yet, about the rest of us for instance.'

'I thought this a natural stop, the first child coming to fruition. Otherwise a diary could go on for ever, like the Bible.'

'But it's nearly all about Nic, makes her seem the favourite.'

'Only because she was the first to go through the various phases of growing up. Dad and I got all the body blows from Nic and we shall probably be immune to them by the time you've all emerged.'

'But we shall all be psychologically different from her so you shouldn't just stop writing.' Penny is seventeen now and into psychology, among other things.

'I shan't stop writing, not altogether. But I'm an individual too, you know, and life outside is beginning to take over. I see signs of mothers being freed from the kitchen and having careers; a kind of women's liberation coming up.'

'But you can't be *too* liberated, you're our Mum!'

'Maybe not *too* liberated. But don't bank on it, Penny, life is full of surprises.'

THE END